Purpose Now! Series by Delina Fajardo

8 Steps
To Find Your True Purpose

~

*Your Step-by-Step Guide
For Finding Your Passions, Your Purpose,
And Living an Empowered Life!*

By

Delina Fajardo

Congrats on taking your first step towards living your destiny

BY DELINA FAJARDO

Cʒ

Purpose Now! Series

- Purpose Now! Book 1:

  *8 Steps to Find Your True Purpose:
  Your Guide To Living An
  Empowered Life!*

- Purpose Now! Book 2:

  *Who is This Sex For Anyways?
  How to Find Purpose, Intimacy and
  Passion in Your Relationship!*

- Purpose Now! Book 3:

  *Are we Friends or Acquaintances?
  Discovering Your Purpose with
  People!*

DISCLAIMER

This book is presented solely for educational and entertainment purposes. The author and publisher are not offering it as legal, accounting, or other professional services advice. While best efforts have been used in preparing this book, the author and publisher make no representations or warranties of any kind and assume no liabilities of any kind with respect to the accuracy or completeness of the contents and specifically disclaim any implied warranties of merchantability or fitness of use for a particular purpose.

Neither the author nor the publisher shall be held liable or responsible to any person or entity with respect to any loss or incidental or consequential damages caused, or alleged to have been caused, directly or indirectly, by the information or programs contained herein.

The publishers, authors, and any other parties involved in the creation, production, provision of information, or delivery of this book specifically disclaim any responsibility, and shall not be liable for any damages, claims, injuries, losses, liabilities, costs or obligations including any direct, indirect, special, incidental, or consequential damages (collectively known as "Damages") whatsoever and howsoever caused, arising out of, or in connection with, the use or misuse of the book and the information contained within it, whether such Damages arise in contract, tort, negligence, equity, statute law, or by way of any other legal theory. The story and its characters and entities are fictional. Any likeness to actual persons, either living or dead, is strictly coincidental.

You may NOT give away, share or resell this intellectual property in any way.

Published by Delina Fajardo.

ACKNOWLEDGEMENTS

First and foremost I want to thank and acknowledge my Creator. My connection with you God is by far the most important thing to me in life. I respect my divine identity, it's lineage, and connection to you. Without you, my life experiences could not be possible. This book and the entire Purpose Now series is an example of what is possible when I stay in faith. Thank you for leading me down a path to serve your mission through my purpose. Thank you for holding me when I cried and celebrating me when I strived. May the results of this book be part of your grander plan!

This book is dedicated to my grandparents Daniel Zorrilla and Mercedes Fajardo. Words on paper cannot express the love, respect and gratitude that I have for you. Thank you for showing me and giving me the love, nurturance, support, respect, appreciation, and prayers. You live in my heart. Thank you for giving and showing me unconditional love.

I want to thank my family and friends. From the bottom of my heart, thank you for loving me unconditionally. Thank you for your support and giving me the motivation that I needed. I'm a loner by nature and can hibernate in the mountains without a problem, but it's with your presence that I am able to magnify my experience of love, laughter and connection. You give me a better quality of life. I appreciate that you give me the space to grow and blossom without judgment. Thank you for all of your love, encouragement, trust and respect. You stood by my side with ALL my change. You embraced it with open arms and went with the flow anticipating my next growth phase. Awe, I love you guys! ☺

Thank you Matthew Coullier for your unconditional love, support and standing by my side through my ups and downs. You took the heat more than anybody else during this process and you deserve the reward of most endured. I respect your relentless strength of enduring my emotional waves. Thank you for being grounded and a pillar of strength. You will always have a special place within my heart. *Nom-Nom! Wilson! Birdface!*

A book like this doesn't happen overnight or alone, neither do dreams, usually. I would like to thank my life-long friend for his invaluable input, feedback, encouragement, motivation, excitement, and friendship along the way. *Thank you, John McCue Jr.!*

I want to thank my mentor and employer Anthony Robbins and everybody on staff at Robbins Research International, especially the team of coaches for your ongoing support. The team is unique in that it feels like a family unit. Thank you to our coaching director Marc Von Musser. You saw my gift and provided me with the space to step into my greatness. You empowered, respected, trusted and guided me. With each Robbins event, Power Team call and Mentoring Call, I transformed into who I am today. It was all in divine time. My involvement with this team was part of my destiny and a vehicle for me to serve my purpose. Through the mission, I found my empowered identity and purpose in life. I am eternally grateful to be part of this team.

I have never experienced such an empowering workplace for growth. It's supportive, encouraging, fun, and selfless with the intention to serve the greater good by empowering and transforming lives. I'm so happy and fulfilled to serve the same mission in changing the world. No organization is perfect, but to walk away from a Robbins event filled with love and happiness says a lot about the organization and its intention. I'm proud to be here! Thank you for your support, encouragement, connection, contribution, and providing the unique space for me to step into whom I really am.

A HUGE thank you to my coaching clients. It is with pleasure and purpose that I serve you. You have helped me experience the magic that exists when like-minded people join for the purpose of transformation. There is nothing else like it. Our union is not by coincidence. Everything has a divine order and right timing to serve the greater good. In many ways you are my teachers. I have learned from you just as much as you have from me. The insights from my coaching come as a result of your commitment and dedication to yourself. Thank you for showing up open and trustful, anticipating your next breakthrough and excited to continue your journey with me. Thank you for allowing me the opportunity to step into my purpose and identity with each session.

DEDICATION

 C33

Purpose + Passion = Fulfillment

I believe that without finding and living your purpose
you cannot be completely fulfilled.

The goal in life is to find your ultimate edge,
live with passion,
and contribute back to others.

This will create sustained fulfillment.

Everybody has a purpose and was created
to do something spectacular.

What is your purpose?
What were you created to do?
True fulfillment comes when you can align yourself
with your purpose.

Find your passion!
Live your purpose!

Be Fulfilled!

CONTENTS

INTRODUCTION

Who I am and What This Book is About

Important Questions

IF YOU PICKED up this book, you might be wondering if there is an easy, time efficient and 100% proven way to finding passion, purpose and fulfillment in life.

You might also:

- Be unsure what to do "when you grow up"
- Be unclear what direction to take
- Be frustrated by the direction your life is going
- Feel that you're not living up to your fullest potential
- Feel stressed by societal pressures to go down a specific path
- Be unhappy with your current career or studies

- Want to change but you're fearful since so much time and money has already been invested
- Use the excuse "not enough time" to pursue my passions or dreams
- Feel that you do not have enough financial security to support living your passions
- Be fearful of the unknown
- Be fearful of vulnerability
- Be fearful of failure or success
- Not know what motivates or drives you
- Have difficulty re-inventing yourself
- Need a specific plan or strategy to follow for transition from career "A" to career "B"
- Be unhappily living a life based on others' expectations, but not your dream
- Be wondering why your success and achievements are not equating to fulfillment

For any or all of the above, this book is for you! In addition, this book is for you if you don't know or consciously realize what your unique skills or talents are. This book is for you if you feel that your life is meant for more, but you don't have a clue what that is or how to get there.

This book is for you if you suffer from taking too many directions and therefore lack clarity and focus on what matters most, or have too many aspirations to accomplish and spin out of control, only exhausting yourself. I call this the hamster on crack, spinning in an endless wheel, utilizing valuable energy without finding resolve or satisfaction.

This book is for you if you suffer from negative beliefs and inner voices that shout at you and prevent you from moving forward.

What This Book is About

This book is about finding your true purpose in life. It is a tool to guide you towards a path of happiness and fulfillment. It is a step-by-step guide to serve as your map and strategy to reconnect you with your authentic identity, passions and purpose.

Each of us has a unique, divine purpose to fulfill and contribute in our lifetime. Our purpose is a reflection of our essence and truth. We can fulfill our purpose by using our unique talents and gifts. Your life's purpose is always evolving. All of your life experiences so far have served a purpose to strengthen and guide you towards your true purpose, essence and truth.

It's an illusion that you have a single purpose. That illusion creates stress and frustration. Instead, the goal is to find your purpose now, which has always been there and still waiting for you. When we find and acknowledge it then we become world changers and 'active agents' for love, peace, and harmony. It is with our unique purpose that we are able raise our vibration and change the world. In my opinion, the goal of is to find your true purpose and to give your heart and soul to it!

Who am I?

And why should you listen to anything I have to say about finding purpose?

I experienced all of it, all of the above! My name is Delina Fajardo. By trade, I'm a Physician Assistant in the Emergency Department. I have worked in various specialties of medicine for the past 15 years. I am also a Certified Life Coach and Peak Performance Results Coach with Anthony Robbins.

You may already know me from my medical or coaching background. Or maybe you know me from reading my blogs; a fan on my Facebook page, *Coach Delina*; visited my website, www.delinafajardo.com; or even stayed as a guest at my vacation rental property Grand View Escapes in Lake Placid, NY.

What you don't know about me is that this book is a result of my life experiences. I didn't realize it at the time but I have been searching for purpose and passion since college. Every single experience was at the right time, right place to bring you this book. My purpose in life is to share the knowledge, wisdom, and strategies that I used to find my true purpose and passion in life.

This book was the reason I had to endure multiple painful experiences, change my medical specialty seven times in ten years and learn everything it takes to strengthen my identity, break through, and land on my feet on the other side. It's my past experiences, along with my education and desire to serve you that gives me the credibility and expertise to guide you towards finding your life's purpose.

You do not need to endure the same struggles that I did to get to the other side. Learn from my mistakes and use my guidance as your tool for happiness and success.

I am able to write this book today because of my strength, wisdom, and lessons learned along the way. Everything happens for a reason. My life experiences had purpose. The purpose of my past experiences was to deliver and share my message through this book. I want to teach you how to find happiness and purpose in your life quicker than I did. Save yourself valuable time and money by learning from my past experiences and mistakes.

My past experiences consisted of many ups and downs. I always felt like I was living a roller coaster ride. My emotional downs consisted of unhappiness, frustration, anger, depression, stress and overwhelm. My emotional ups were temporary and mostly related to being successful, "buying happiness", feeling significant, status and money.

I can tell you that I have been there and it was extremely frustrating for me because I kept pushing forward instead of simply allowing. I kept pushing "the boulder" that resisted. I am, by definition, an over-achiever, so the only way I knew best how to achieve success was to compete and conquer.

Have you ever worked really hard towards trying to achieve something but got to the finish line and was disappointed by how little happiness and fulfillment you experienced? I have been at that finish line multiple times, where I felt achievement but anticipated much more satisfaction as a result of my strides and efforts. Most of us are programmed with the mindset that achievement brings fulfillment. And it becomes disheartening once you realize that your achievements didn't reap the rewards that you anticipated.

Up until two years ago, my accumulated achievements were many but I still lacked fulfillment. It was frustrating for me and left me feeling perplexed. One day I finally sat down and got honest with myself. I acknowledged the fact that I changed my specialty seven times in ten years as a Physician Assistant:

1. General Surgery,
2. Cardio-Thoracic Surgery,
3. Mesotherapy,
4. Plastic Surgery,
5. Emergency Medicine,
6. Urgent Care,
7. Alcohol & Drug Detox/Psychiatry,
8. and then back to Emergency Medicine.

People might change their career path twice in a lifetime but I did so *seven times in a decade*! I also acknowledged the fact that I had lived in multiple locations from East to West Coast and was nonetheless still searching. I was bummed by these realizations because I knew - I just knew - that I was running. I was running away each and every single time.

So I started to ask myself, "What are you looking for, what do you really want? What will make you happy?

Ironically, I thought that I obtained everything to sustain happiness already- security, certainty, comfort, and financial stability – and I worked hard to get there. I had a house, a car, furniture, and a supportive, loving boyfriend; what else could I want? What did I really need?

Then I got it! I really knew this time because I had chest pain. It hurt. My heart ripped open and it was like having an Aha moment on steroids. It brought me to tears. I was feeling vulnerable and guilty for not listening to my inner voice sooner as it shouted:

LOVE, HAPPINESS, FULFILLMENT!

LOVE, HAPPINESS, FULFILLMENT!

LOVE, HAPPINESS, and FULFILLMENT!

I was expecting the voice to say money, success, warmer weather, or a new car - that might have been easier to accept.

I had finally given myself permission to open up, listen, and reveal what mattered most. It was a great celebratory moment of connection with myself that lasted all of about eleven minutes before I started stressing with the "how-to's:"

- How do I get that?

- What do I need to do differently?
- Where do I start?
- Do I really want change after ALL the time and money invested into my career already?
- What type of career and lifestyle will meet these needs?
- Can I afford to make the change?
- I already have a set lifestyle; can I financially support it?

And so my journey began!

Here are the building blocks that got me started:

1) The wisdom and the passion in my heart
2) A compelling vision
3) Acquired skills and abilities

That is what you need to start this journey. The rest we will discover, together along the way. Allow the steps of this book to navigate you. Remember to trust yourself and the journey. Listen to your heart and inner wisdom.

As you read the chapters of this book, understand that these are designed as a step-by-step approach. These steps are in chronological order and designed to be followed in sequence for distinctions, breakthroughs, and transformations to occur. I have lived the experience and tested it over and over again with clients. And it works! Each step will lead you towards your path of purpose.

If you want to live a life ignited by passion and purpose, then you're ready for this book. By the end of your experience, you will live more passionately, love more fully, and contribute your natural born gifts to the world. Give yourself permission to open through love instead of remaining closed by fear.

PURPOSE & PASSION

*"If you don't design your own life plan,
chances are you'll fall into someone else's plan.
And guess what they have planned for you?
Not much."~ Jim Rohn*

Welcome!

WELCOME TO YOUR NEW OPPORTUNITY for living with purpose and passion! It's an opportunity all of us have, yet so few are aware of or realize. As you embark upon this three-volume series I really hope that my voice comes through and we connect personally because, yes, I'm an author, but that is secondary to my own passion and purpose as a coach.

I've been there. I know and understand what you've been through, what you need and what you want. My story and life experiences are proof that finding purpose and passion comes from getting out of your head, and going back into your heart.

In addition to my book you now have access to my blogs, videos, and other helpful tools to give you the insights you'll need to truly create your own destiny of passion and purpose. Take advantage of the tools on my website, including your free personalized profile assessment - *Living Your Purpose*. You can even take it a step further with coaching sessions (see the back of the book for details).

Really Doing It

This is not an ordinary self-help tome, rather we – you and I – are about to roll up our sleeves together and actually change your life. You in turn can change the lives of those around you. We can create a better world by first being the change ourselves. We will do this with insights and actual exercises, so I'm asking you right here and right now, right where you are, to commit to your journey. It's one many never set out on, unfortunately, but you have such a chance right here and now.

Commit to improving your life, to making it one of fulfillment by combining purpose and passion!

- Are you living your dreams?

- Are you connected to your passions?

- Are you acting on your ideas?

- Are you doing all that you can do?

- Are you excited about your day or feel bored and stuck?

Your Birthright

Many of us believe that living our passions and desires is out of our reach. We think that we are just not smart enough, not good enough, or maybe even not worthy enough to live our dreams.

It is your birthright to live your desires!

Let me repeat that while you let it sink in: It is your birthright to live your desires. Heck, it's your duty! You are here to fulfill your purpose in this world. Your desires and passions create the path that leads directly to the fulfillment of that purpose.

We should strive for a life lived with passion and purpose. Joy and happiness come when we pursue the moments that light us up. When we do what we love and give freely of ourselves, what we offer comes back to us beyond our imagination. There are no limits to what we can give and receive. My mission is to help you find your unique gifts, live authentically and find your purpose. Come with me and you'll discover who you really are, why you're here, and what you're meant to do.

After all, that's exactly what I do each day; I help others find their paths. That's my purpose, and my passion, and I can tell you therein lies the formula for your own meaningful success – in fact a higher level of success than just money:

Purpose + Passion = Fulfillment

If I told you that you can experience lasting change towards success and fulfillment, would you be willing to put forth the effort? There is no better time than right now to live passionately in every area of your life.

In this series, I want you to just imagine that I'm right there with you, because I am. I will ask a lot of questions that will lead you to the answers you have been seeking possibly all of your life.

Questions & Answers

All you have to do is let the answers bubble to the surface, often effortlessly. At times there will be obstructions for you to remove, but the answers will appear and you will be wiser and happier for them.

Listen as they come. No more excuses. For instance, what simply appears in your mind when I ask about your own identity?

Who are you?

And when we look for what gets you passionate, what answers arise as I ask:

What motivates you?

Fascinating, isn't it? We can even touch on your higher purpose(s) by asking:

Why are you here?

Everyone I ask those questions of has answers. That is partly the magic of coaching and changing lives: I have the questions and you have the answers. Answer these for yourself. Take your time, and realize we are just getting started!

What does it mean to live a life of purpose and passion?

Why is it important? Who benefits?

Believe it or not, I care about you. You might wonder how I can say that so boldly because more than likely we've never actually met, and I am not telepathically receiving your answers, am I? The truth is my passion has led me to doing just what I am doing with you now. We are having a bit of what many writers describe as "telepathy by book." Rather than a phone call or otherwise live meeting we will accomplish great things over this series of three books.

And I actually know quite a bit about you already. If you're reading this book, for example, you will have a lot in common with me as well as my friends and clients (although that line gets happily blurred pretty quickly!)

Trust me, I do understand what it's like to live unhappily without passion or purpose. I do understand an unfulfilling life and ups and downs. I very much understand wanting more from life and the undeniable hope that a more fulfilling path exists – where each of us shares our unique gifts. I also understand what it takes to bring that out in me and in you. I've done it and I see it done all the time.

I can't tell you how excited I am to have this opportunity with you now – to share the insights that will take you to a higher level of being and a more fulfilling existence!

Again, take your time and just lightly and to yourself answer the following:

- What is most important in your life?

- What is the primary focus of your life?

- What is the story you have been telling yourself?

- Why do you do what you do?

- What are some events that shaped your life?

If you have opened yourself to your own answers, congratulations! There are many more to come. I have organized this first important volume into actual steps – not chapters – and we can take them together, I am your gentle but insistent guide. Read on! And I am very happy to point out that you have just now, already taken your first baby steps to truly leading a life of purpose, passion, and fulfillment, right here in this brief introduction! So once again, welcome, and bon voyage!

STEP 1: IDENTITY FIRST

Align With Your Authentic Identity

Inspired Insight:
*"It's in the alignment with your authentic identity
that connects you with your purpose."* ~ *Coach Delina*

IT IS MY DESIRE in this chapter to help you re-align with your authentic identity. Your authentic identity is your empowered source of inner strength, clarity and vitality. Once you re-align with this part of you, you can spontaneously fulfill your hearts desires and enjoy the abundance of miracles everyday. This first step is vital towards finding and living your purpose effortlessly.

I will guide you on a path to align with this identity so that you can get a glimpse of how you need to show up to live an empowered life. In my opinion, everything starts with identity! Your life experiences are determined by your identity first!

The goal is to re-align with the authentic part of you that is naturally empowered. Through empowered identity you will discover a new voice and speak your truth in ways you've never done before. You will find your inner strength and confidence. This authentic identity knows your truth and has the answers to all of your questions. It provides you with the clarity and wisdom that you need. Most importantly, it will help you discover your purpose or Dharma. Alignment with this identity will open up the path towards to your purpose driven destiny.

It's time to discover:
- Who you really are
- Why you're here

In this chapter you will:

- Unleash your Super Hero
- Be guided through a step-by-step alignment exercise,
- And, most importantly, you will understand the importance *identity first* is for making decisions, taking action, and finding one's purpose.

By the end:

1. You will have strategies to re-align,
2. Understand the massive value of realignment for empowered living,
3. You will make three empowering decisions towards change and creating your destiny,
4. And you will develop a daily ritual to condition and embody your new identity.

Read with an open heart and mind to allow for the infinite possibilities available through your deep-seeded wisdom. I encourage you to develop NEW insights and empowering beliefs. Give yourself permission and allow yourself to detach from the old thoughts patterns that prevent you from being your very best.

Alignment

My belief is that we are born aligned with our authentic identity. The challenge is that our surroundings typically do not support us to remain in our alignment; therefore it is our responsibility to re-align with our identity daily. Once we do, we can start living authentically happy.

Through my work, I have the privilege of speaking to clients from different continents, religions, social status and professions. With this opportunity and gift, I became resourceful in gaining insight for the foundation of this chapter. I was curious how others defined ALIGNMENT.

It seems to be a simple word to define, but what I found is that the interpretation dramatically changed between strangers, family members and clients. In response to my question, "Are you aligned?" some actual responses were:

"Why do you ask?"
"What is it?"
"Will I have to stretch?"
"What are you trying to sell me?"
"Are you related to the vacuum guy that came yesterday?"
"My car is old; I should get brakes before an alignment"
"Can my friend Shelly come?"
"Can I bring my cat?"

"Isn't there a pill for this?"

"Are you making fun of how I walk?"

"How do I get it?"

"How much does it cost?"

"Does Wal-Mart sell it?"

"How do I know when I have it? Will someone tell me, because I do hear voices from time to time."

"Do you have an infomercial?"

"Do I have to shave my head?"

"Why do it?"

"Who does it?"

"Does it involve pins being inserted into body parts?"

"Will I need to lie down on a couch? Is the couch leather? I sweat when I sit on leather, will that affect the coaching?"

"What are the benefits?"

"Do I need medical insurance? Because I don't have any, is that a problem?"

"Are there side effects?"

And my personal favorite, "Can you tell that I'm stoned?"

The truth is that most people don't understand alignment or how to achieve it. When I refer to *alignment* I mean the action of centering yourself and going within. The intention is to find your inner wisdom to search for the answers that you seek.

Most times we barely spend ten minutes a day in stillness just being present with our body and breath. Everybody has attention deficit disorder these days. It's not hard to figure out why this is happening, considering all the technology devices available and our desire to get in touch with the world. The problem is that the more you get "in touch" with the world, the less you are "in touch" with yourself. Going within is like a foreign language to many people. It's scary and uncertain.

I will cut to the chase on this one, nobody really wants to spend the time to go within and reflect because of underlying fears and beliefs that they are not capable or worthy enough to find solutions to their problems. There is a lack of confidence and trust within. This coupled with the fact that it's too easy to seek the answers externally causes pointless chatter on the worldwide web.

We are all guilty of taking the easy way out and taking a pill, consuming an energy drink, buying countless books and audio products, taking numerous tests, signing up for every webinar and event - all to seek answers that we don't have. Or do we?

We are programmed to believe that the answers are found in the external world and not from within. I support everything and anything for educational purposes, but I believe there is a balance. There is a point when you must find the answers with your own wisdom; otherwise you're addicted to the "must have" and the "gotta have."

The problem with solely relying on others or the external world for answers is that the external world is commercial; built on capitalistic ideas. Chances are you will be easily misled and misguided down a path that doesn't really serve you. You may think that you "need" it or "must have" it. But without proper alignment and good judgment, it's possible that you may lack the sensory acuity to know the difference. Although the vision portrayed in advertisements all around is convincing by offering a compelling future, it doesn't mean that we need to fall into the false perceptions that are portrayed.

Instead, look within to create a destiny from your internal realm. Everything you need is within you right now! This is your life, your race and your time. Do not allow the external world to design your destiny. Find the compelling vision from within and create that one. You have what it takes! You have the answers. Happiness is a mindset and not found from the external world or external factors.

It's time to unleash your authentic identity and unlock the answers that lie within you. The more you play full out using this book, the more chances you have of reaching your goals.

Where there is an exercise, take the time to complete it. We are shaping your destiny and each step is designed in sequential order to create the breakthroughs you need for your success! Skipping out on an exercise is cheating yourself of what you'll need moving forward.

Let's begin!

What does alignment mean to you? What does it look like? Do any sounds come to mind? How does it feel? Write your answers here:

_____

_____

_____

_____

_____

_____

_____

Correct!

Congratulations! Your answer represents your alignment to your authentic identity. It is a preview of the ways you can reconnect to who you really are. It represents the meanings, visions, sounds and feelings that support the alignment to your authentic identity.

It should be celebrated because from this place you are most resourceful. It didn't take you long, but you took the time to go within and reflect on your answer based on your core beliefs, and not based by what your saw on *Real Housewives* or *Duck Dynasty*.

Alignment to your authentic identity is a feeling of connection to yourself. When you lose alignment, you lose the connection to who you really are.

The most common age group that struggles with finding this connection and their authentic identity are teenagers. This is certainly a time in life when identity crisis is at its peak as teenagers struggle with self-esteem.

They tend to go with what's popular instead of what's right. This reminds me of my early tendency for neon belts, weatherproof hair, and denim in the 80's. By the way, I do recall all of those making contemporary strides again.

Teenagers will sacrifice their sense of connection to themselves in order to fit in and be liked. Most teenagers seek love, connection and significance. They will try to meet their needs through fashion trends or more dangerous measures such as sex and drugs.

It is not breaking news that teenage girls today are trying to meet their needs for love and connection through sex. They establish their identity through popularity, which is usually rated by their clothes, body and sexual activity. They connect sexual activity with recognition, acknowledgment, significance, and identity. They do not realize that it actually takes away from their authentic identity more than anything else.

My message to teens is that your virginity is part of your empowered identity- pure, vibrant, and sacred. Don't give away your empowerment so easily. You risk feeling disempowered when you "give it up." God bless teenagers because we have all been there, and it's a confusing time.

As teenagers struggle with finding their identity, adults struggle with remembering it.

Again, my belief is that we are all born with alignment and a hunch of what our purpose is. As "life happens," we lose alignment and insight of this purpose. Most importantly, when alignment is missing, we lose insight of our identity and personal power.

Our next step is to practice re-alignment with your empowered identity and teach you an easy and effective ritual to re-align daily. Alignment should become a daily practice and ritual in order to strengthen your inner wisdom.

Let's take a step back for a moment, drop the industry terms and just listen to a recent story about my lifelong friend: A story of a man who is definitely out of alignment.

My friend in his 30's, is a handsome bachelor in New York City who has a good but very stressful job, makes respectable money, lives a healthy lifestyle, loves sports, has a house in the suburbs, has a fairly new car, is an animal lover, and likes to travel, yet rarely does.

He is humorous and can captivate the whole room when he tells a story. However, he works long hours and seems to live to work instead of working to live. He used to make the most of his time, but lately has fallen into a rut and always seems to be playing catch up. Sound familiar?

My friend "appears" to be happy. He always sports a smile, dates when he can, has a solid financial future, and spends his free time paying bills, running errands, working on his house and watching sports. Except, he is constantly fighting with his roommate.

His roommate is quite different than what you're expecting. She is a six-week old, ball of anger he named Fea (FAI-ah).

Fea is Spanish for ugly. It may sound rude at first, but I have seen this feline, and her name is fitting. From the start, the relationship with his "roommate" was a contentious one and when asked how he and his new pet were getting along he stated, "I'll put it this way, we respect each other's distance."

Some months had passed before we reconnected this past July on a beautiful 85-degree New York summer afternoon, a perfect day for enjoying the outdoors. When I spoke to my friend about how his day was spent he said, "Well, I just finished fighting with the cat so now I have to hurry up and cut the lawn so I can go running."

I couldn't believe what I was hearing and had to ask more about this fight. He continued, "She doesn't know how to act. She kills everything in the yard, she's dirty and stays out for days, and when she is home she is disrespectful, swipes at me and is forever hissing. I think she needs Jesus."

To me, this was just a typical alpha-male moment between him and a mammal that spends 78% of its time sleeping and apparently the other 22% hunting and being "disrespectful."

Laughing, I asked how long this "argument" lasted and he replied, "40 minutes." This man wasted FORTY MINUTES of valuable time on a beautiful day arguing with a cat named Fea! And he thinks that the cat doesn't know how to act?

Now, it is possible that this animal needs some sort of intervention, whether GOD or cat Ritalin, but my friend definitely needs alignment!

My point of sharing this story is to acknowledge how easily we can become misaligned. Life stressors are the usual culprit. Increased stressors from work, bills, household duties or family responsibilities can consume our lives to the point that we start believing in the false illusion that our self-sabotaging patterns are part of life. Self-sabotaging is a sign it's time to re-align!

Step #1
Unleash the Super Hero

Can you remember a time when you felt completely certain and empowered?

A time when you were unstoppable? A time when nothing could prevent you from doing what you set out to do?

You had the solution, because YOU WERE the solution. You made decisions quickly and effortlessly. You had certainty, energy and vitality.

Everybody has moments when they felt like a Super Hero. What was yours?

Visualize that moment closer and brighter. What was different about it? Did you walk differently? How did you feel?

More importantly, what could you create and make happen? What impact did you have on yourself and others? What did you believe about yourself?

That is the empowered identity you should be operating from daily. Have you been living with this person in control? Have you been living from this identity? This is an invitation to re-align with the Super Hero within. We all have a part of our identity that is a Super Hero. Are you ready to find yours?

Who is the Super Hero within you?

Can you remember as a child identifying yourself as your favorite super hero? Who was it? Superman, Batman, Wonder Woman, Spiderman, The Incredible Hulk, Captain America, Hercules, Aquaman? What did you identify with most about that hero? Whatever you identified mostly with, is really a part of your identity too.

It is time to unleash the Super Hero within!

It's time to create your destiny and live your purpose.

Super Hero Exercise:

(Safety note: This Super Hero Exercise is a rhetorical one only and is for the purpose of an inner intellectual awakening. Do not squeeze into some Spandex and tie a table cloth around your neck looking to pick up heavy shit or leap tall buildings in a single bound.)

Close your eyes, sit up straight, take a few deep breaths and visualize that you are that super hero now. Most likely, you can immediately snap into that identity because it is already a part of you and it's ready to be unleashed. Invite this part of you to reveal and unleash. Feel the empowerment from within.

How does this super hero stand? Scan your body and notice the position of your head, chin and shoulders. Find your center of gravity and take a deep breath. Visualize a beam of light and vitality entering the top of your head and exiting out through your feet, anchoring you to earth's surface. Your head is light and lifted off your shoulders. Sit with that for a moment. How does it feel?

With this strong posture, take a deep breath and focus on what you believe about yourself as this Super Hero.

Does anything prevent this Super Hero? Are challenges a problem for this Super Hero? Can this person dominate and accomplish anything they set their mind to? Can this identity perceive obstacles as simply opportunities for triumph?

Can you relate to this part of you? Maybe you can visualize yourself with a red cape - taking names, chewing bubble gum and kicking butt!

This identity is within all the time BUT you need to re-align to it? When you connect to this identity regularly and condition it, it becomes automatic. Give your empowered identity a nickname - a Super Hero nickname that is fun and outrageous. Labeling it with a nickname acknowledges this part of you and allows you to call it when needed.

My super hero nickname is: _____

What do you believe about yourself as this claimed identity? (ie. I can do anything I set my mind to)

_____

_____

_____

List words that describe yourself: (ie. funny, courageous, confident)

_____

_____

_____

List emotions you may feel: (ie. empowered, love, passion, freedom)

_____

_____

_____

What are three goals that you can make for this week?

1. _____

2. _____

3. _____

What action steps are needed for those goals?

_____

_____

_____

What commitments do you need to make?

_____

_____

_____

Step #2
Create rituals.

Make a conscious effort to re-align everyday so that you can connect with your true potential and power.

Throughout history we have witnessed many fall short of achieving their goals, yet others with similar obstacles manifest their dreams. The secret is the application of rituals.

If you want to model someone who is successful, follow their rituals.

All leaders, professional athletes and others alike have rituals to consistently achieve their goals. Establishing a ritual is the best way to provide the structure needed to change a habit or to create a new one.

- A *habit* is an acquired pattern of behavior that often occurs automatically.

- A *ritual* is an action or series of action steps that are consistently repeated in a predetermined way.

When creating a ritual for living empowered daily, it is important to connect with the feelings and emotions associated with an empowered identity.

Our emotions control our wellbeing and the quality of our lives. Where do you USUALLY go emotionally? What is your emotional habit? Do you become Stuart Smalley or Debbie Downer? Be aware of your emotions, and how they shape your present moment.

In the Super Hero exercise, you listed emotions that were connected to your empowered identity. Your daily ritual should include the opportunity to feel and connect to those emotions.

Your emotions can serve as your navigation tool.

Let's use *gratitude* as an example.

If gratitude was one of your listed emotions then you want to create a ritual that gets you into a state of gratitude daily. This way you are creating a ritual that results in the emotion of gratitude. It's easier to create a habit if the ritual produces an emotion that you want to feel.

Love as an example

If love was an emotion, think about all the ways that you consistently express love for yourself and others. How can you consistently experience love daily? The ritual should result in feeling the emotion.

Confidence as an example

If confidence was an emotion, think about a ritual that would evoke the emotion of confidence. An example might be to list your top strengths. The top 10 reasons why you are awesome! Do a different list daily.

This is your life and you have the choice whether you want to live it empowered or not. Sometimes it is doing something simple at the start of your day that makes all the difference. Try setting your phone alarm with a favorite song that evokes your desired emotion; twice if you want to remind yourself to re-connect. Try waking up 30 minutes earlier with the intention to go within in any way that feels right that morning. Take the time to reconnect and re-align. Maybe it's reading, meditating, writing, dancing, praying, going for a walk, exercising. Even if it's just looking out the window, spend the time to re-align. This time will set the tempo and pace of your day. It will give you clarity and focus. You will leap over your hurdles feeling energized.

Identity first is the solution to stress, fatigue, exhaustion, confusion, insecurity and poor judgment. Only by placing identity first can we truly trust our own decisions.

Everything in life requires a decision.

Everything requires a decision, and our decisions determine our outcome. It is in the moment of our decisions that we shape our path and destiny.

Every decision made has impact and influences your life. Empowered decisions manifest an empowered destiny. More often than not, we make decisions under suboptimal physical, mental, and emotional conditions. Many times, we are making decisions in a disempowered identity, while under pressure.

What happens to your physical body when you need to make a decision while under pressure? Do you feel your chest or throat tighten up? Tingling in your face or hands? Do you lose your ability to speak effectively? Do you lose clarity and focus? Do you shut down?

How effective are your decisions from this disempowered identity? Think about a decision that you made while in a suboptimal or inferior state. How many infomercial purchases do you regret? How many "must-have" health juicers, pajama jeans or Ab-Rollers can there possibly be? Okay, maybe you didn't buy the pajama jeans, but what about all of your impulse buys at the cash register? I am guilty of buying candy in a Pez dispenser.

It is your responsibility to come from a place of empowerment while your making decisions if you want to have good judgment. Decisions made while aligned in your empowered state are typically the right ones.

In summary, we are born with an empowered identity and a purpose to serve in a unique way. We are witnessing evolution entering into a phase of awakening. It is our responsibility to step up with our authentic empowered identity and contribute to the world instead of watching from the sidelines. We should have the intention to positively influence others and make a difference. You are being called to contribute your unique gifts through your purpose.

Using your authentic identity equips you as an "active agent" to make a greater difference. Use every opportunity to do so. Everything you need is within. We are living at the edge of the greatest awakening humanity has ever experienced. I bet you're living at the edge of your greatness too, otherwise you wouldn't have chosen this book.

Re-live the moments you felt alive, empowered, passionate and like a Super Hero.

Fea

And remember that time passes quickly, so don't waste a minute of it arguing with a cat.

"Alignment is happiness and connection with higher self and divinity"
~ Delina Fajardo

STEP 2: BEING GRATEFUL

A state of BEing not DOing

Inspired Insight:
"Getting into a state of gratitude is the single most powerful tool to manifest your dreams." ~ *Coach Delina*

BEING GRATEFUL MEANS being in a state of gratitude if you want to live your purpose. Gratitude opens your heart and leads to your passions and purpose. If you want to fulfill your desires by living your life's purpose, you must practice being grateful.

Gratitude is one of the greatest virtues to ascertain. It is the single most important way to manifest your abundance.

How often are you grateful? Are you in a state of gratitude daily? Do you resist yourself from either giving or receiving gratitude? Do you know how to practice BEing grateful?

I have encountered some people with conflicting feelings about gratitude. Some think that they need to be "spiritual" in order to experience gratitude; they associate gratitude with a spiritual practice. I have also noticed that many people feel unworthy and undeserving of feeling the emotion of gratitude. And most often I hear people say that they need an incentive before they can be grateful.

Gratitude is a state of BEing and not a state of DOing. It is important to know that you can feel gratitude and be grateful without feeling the need to earn the emotion through a task or an obligation.

Putting expectations on yourself and others to "deliver first" before BEing grateful will only create unhappiness and frustration. Your "rules" on when and how you experience gratitude should be evaluated. Let go of all rules that limit your potential to experience gratitude regularly and easily. Those rules will limit your potential for abundance and fulfillment.

Key Elements to Gratitude:

1. It is impossible to be grateful and fearful at the same time.

2. Gratitude is a state of BEing and not a state of DOing.

3. Opportunities for gratitude surround us.

Did you know that it's impossible to feel grateful and fearful at the same time? This is true. Try it out for yourself! Appreciation, gratitude and love are some of the highest emotions one can experience. Fear and anger are the lowest. The good news is that you cannot experience both a very high and low vibrational emotion simultaneously. It is very difficult to bring the emotion of anger into your body while feeling gratitude. You would literally have to focus your attention on something that makes you feel angry for an extended period of time. And why would you want to do that? Being grateful is the antidote to feeling negative emotions.

The trick is to focus on feeling gratitude to negate your feelings of anger, fear, anxiety, or overwhelm. Practice by stacking moments of gratitude during times of distress.

Gratitude is a state of BEing and not a state of DOing. This simply means that the state gratitude doesn't require a checklist of accomplishments prior to experiencing it. It doesn't require an action step or an accomplished task. Be careful not to get caught up in the DOing or your "things to do."

Gratitude as a state of being means to listen, observe, and embrace your surroundings; notice your present moment. The secret is to stay connected and JUST BE in your present moment while embracing the beauty, sounds and the people that surround you. Get connected to your state of BEing.

The last key element to gratitude is knowing that life, and all your experiences, brings endless chances to be grateful. In each moment we are given opportunity for gratitude. Many magic moments and opportunities to experience gratitude are missed.

The essence of gratitude is all around us. Consider how effortlessly and easily some of these gifts of abundance show up. It may appear as a penny on the floor, a hug, or a smile.

The difference is what you notice and what you ignore. When you see a penny on the floor, what does it mean to you? What could it mean to connect a feeling of gratitude?

Take notice of how much gratitude surrounds you. You will be pleasantly surprised by the multitude of gifts that continue to appear throughout your day and for days to come. There are many opportunities available, yet we rarely take the time to experience them. As one of the greatest and highly sought virtues, it is surprising how we tend to dismiss being grateful.

I feel compelled to speak to those that cannot find a reason to be grateful everyday. Because I'm a straight shooter I will be blunt with you – you are simply focusing on the wrong thing. A common mistake is the habit of expectations. If, for whatever reason, you place expectations or become attached to an expectation then you're focusing on the wrong thing; this sets you up for disappointment. It will become difficult to experience gratitude if your outcome doesn't manifest exactly as planned. It is easier to experience gratitude if you're grateful for the journey itself, regardless of the outcome.

We have too many established rules around why, how and when we can experience gratitude. Instead, simply 'just be' in a state of gratitude and live through an open heart.

Change your expectations to appreciation and gratitude follows.

Appreciate what you have NOW in order to duplicate your abundance, fulfillment and blessings. In order for us to truly experience everything the universe has to offer, we must first come to appreciate all that we already have. By simply saying "thank you," for all that you have, you open the door to further opportunity and abundance.

A simple yet powerful gratitude prayer that I use is:
"Thank you for this life,
thank you for my existence,
thank you for my experiences."

Gratitude in our daily lives is transformational. It can turn scarcity into abundance and fear into love. As we focus on the things that we are grateful for, we are essentially appreciating and accepting our life as is.

The highest level of gratitude is an appreciation of our existence. When we sincerely thank God for our existence and appreciate ourselves "as delivered", we experience the highest level of gratitude. As you move towards gratitude an opening shifts within the heart. Take the time to embrace the feelings of deep gratitude. It's the ultimate training process to manifest what you want. If you stack feelings of gratitude, every cell in your body will heal and transform.

Gratitude during hardship

Finding gratitude during hardship is more powerful than during moments of celebration. The real lessons of life come from our challenges. In fact, our challenges will have the greatest lessons within them. Problems will always exist, don't expect not to have them. What you want to expect is a better quality problem.

If you are called to a higher purpose and your vision aligns with God's design, then your problems are meant for your growth. If you change your perception of a problem then you will be happier. You need to perceive a problem as a lesson, not as a challenge. Be grateful for your problems. Problems exist to teach you how to manifest the greater part of yourself. Problems aren't meant to prevent you, but more to stretch you from your comfort zone and help you grow. Problems are also an opportunity for you to create solutions for your next problem, learning from past experiences. The biggest challenge is recognizing the lesson within the problem. If you choose to ignore the lesson and not grow from it, it's bound to repeat.

Have you noticed re-occurring "patterns" in your life that show up over and over again? The pattern repeats because the lesson wasn't learned. You need to be aware of the lesson, learn from it and grow, otherwise it just repeats.

Do not get caught up in thinking "Why is this happening *to* me?"

Problems happen *for* you, not *to* you. Don't play the "victim" card:

- "I am a victim of my past experiences."
- "I am a victim of my circumstances."

We have all lived through unfortunate experiences, everyone has had difficulties, and everybody has experienced pain and suffering. Focus on the positive impacts that resulted from those painful experiences.

Ask Yourself:

- What am I supposed to learn from this?
- How can I use this lesson to improve my life or serve others?

If you're having trouble finding the lesson then you might be caught up *in* the problem instead of having a birds-eye view. Consider what you can be grateful for despite the unfortunate situation. Lessons need to be learned to reach your next stage of growth. Each stage serves as a stepping-stone in the journey of your life.

Did you know?

Michael Jordan and Bob Cousy were each cut from their high school basketball teams. Jordan once observed, "I've missed more than 9000 shots in my career. I've lost almost 300 games. 26 times, I've been trusted to take the game winning shot and missed. I've failed over and over and over again in my life. And that is why I succeed."

Did you know?

Walt Disney was fired by a newspaper editor because "he lacked imagination and had no good ideas." He went bankrupt several times before he built Disneyland. In fact, the proposed park was originally rejected by the city of Anaheim on the grounds that it would only attract riffraff.

Did you know?

Thomas Edison's teachers said he was "too stupid to learn anything." He was fired from his first two jobs for being "non-productive." As an inventor, Edison made 1,000 unsuccessful attempts at inventing the light bulb. When a reporter asked, "How did it feel to fail 1,000 times?" Edison replied, "I didn't fail 1,000 times. The light bulb was an invention with 1,000 steps."

Successful people don't view problems as obstacles. They re-frame the challenge in their mind so that it becomes a stepping-stone, a lesson and a gift.

They are grateful for learning how to improve for their next attempt and view the experience as needed for their success.

Life happens to everybody for everybody. Our experiences

are a non-stop roller coaster that is not meant to be painful, yet just another experience.

Be grateful for your experiences and the lessons within them.

Find the space in your life to be grateful. Everything you have is a gift. Through gratitude you will feel self-appreciation and self-love and want to share it with others. Give yourself permission to feel worthy of gratitude. Take the time to enjoy present moments of gratitude. Take the time to appreciate your loved ones.

BEing grateful every day

Daily appreciation will enhance your awareness of the all blessings that surround you. Be grateful for everything you can see, hear or feel, for whatever weather greets you, for your family, for your significant other, for nature, clean air and the outdoors, for the food on your table, for good hair days, because your boss took his meds, for the voices in your head - regardless of the language, for the dog that chased you up the driveway, for the last Twinkie, for mouthwash, for the last bit of air freshener spray in your friends bathroom after taco night, and for the magical moments that make life a pleasurable mystery.

Get to know your family differently. Appreciate the small things that routinely get taken for granted. Open your eyes to your neighborhood. Take opportunity at stoplights to embrace the surroundings, scenery, community, and people. Embrace your surroundings through awareness.

Keep a gratitude journal.

A great way to stack gratitude is to capture and celebrate. Keeping a gratitude journal is great ritual to remind you of the magic moments that surrounded you. It is an easy tool to bring gratitude into your life.

In summary, being grateful opens your heart and door to infinite possibilities. From a place of sincere gratitude you can cultivate anything and everything. Gratitude is the single most important virtue to have for a fulfilled life. Through gratitude you can manifest your purpose and much more.

STEP 3: DISCOVER YOUR PASSIONS

What Is Your Secret Sauce?

Inspired Insight:
"Don't play small, rise up to your greatest potential everyday in every way!" ~ *Coach Delina*

ARE YOU LIVING your purpose or dreams? Do you spend your day doing the things that you love?

Do others comment on how happy you look and how much fun you are to be around? When you wake up in the morning are you excited about your day? Are you excited about your weekly projects? If not, then you're not connected to your passions and it's time to find your secret sauce!

Your passions are the core ingredients to your secret sauce and lead you directly to your purpose and the expression of your destiny. Furthermore, your living your purpose leads to abundance and infinite opportunity.

When we do anything with passion, we open into the expression of who we really are. In turn, the natural flow and creativity expressed fills us with joy, happiness, inspiration, and love. Our passions serve as a catalyst to living our purpose and being happy.

Simply stated, when we are living through our passions, we are igniting the parts of us that serve purpose. This chapter is to help you identify your secret ingredients and discover your secret sauce – all part of the master plan:

Find Your True Purpose!

Your true purpose is always out there and waiting for you to discover it. All that is required of you is to simply give yourself permission and say YES. It may sound like a no-brainer but many people do not know what drives or motivates them. They forgot what they are passionate about and even feel undeserving to live with passion.

Tell me, what do you enjoy doing for *others* more than anything else? Listen to whatever immediately comes to mind and write it here:

_____

_____

_____

_____

Notice that I asked what you enjoy doing for *others* and not yourself. The purpose was to get your intentional response of will and deed, which ultimately leads to your purpose.

What if I asked, what do *you* enjoy doing? What lights *you* up and makes *you* happy?

_____

_____

_____

_____

Can you appreciate the difference in your responses? Let's use my answers as an example.

To the first question, I respond:

- Inspiring, motivating and encouraging
- Coaching and transforming their life
- Decorating homes; Feng Shui for others

To the second question, I respond:

- Hiking
- Swimming
- Meditating
- Vacation

Tweaking the question to command your brain to respond differently will provoke a better response.

We are not usually equipped to ask ourselves the right questions because we are emotionally involved in "our story".

This is why it's a good idea to hire a certified life coach who has the trained perspective, tools, and strategies. Coaching is my passion and serves as a way for me to live my purpose.

I am at fault for not considering my passions early in my career. Instead, I chose my PA career to meet my needs of financial security and stability. My passions were my strongest resources but I overlooked them as my gifts and natural-born talents. With the amount of time that is spent in the workplace, we should consider incorporating our passions.

Does your career incorporate your passions? If not, what careers do?

Your career should be as fulfilling to you as the paycheck you get from it. The highest paying job is not necessarily the one for you. Who says that you need to travel through life watching the clock from 9-5? That is the result of choosing a career for security, stability, money and significance.

The occupational world has become a very vast and diverse place where you use talents and gifts as your strongest assets towards career fulfillment and enhance the enjoyment of life.

Do not discount your talents and natural gifts as assets. The strongest asset's you have are those that are innate within you. Consider the idiosyncrasies that are distinctive to you and use them to your advantage.

Are you expressing your natural talents daily?

Do you know what your talents are?

What comes naturally to you?

We tend to discount our natural talents and gifts because they are effortless. If we disregard what comes naturally to us then we are disregarding our God given assets. Do not ignore what comes naturally to you and express yourself through your gifts.

Your unique talents will separate you from the competition. Market the heck out of your natural talents. Unique talents are not meant to be conventional, the quirkier the better. Be authentically unique and stand out. These are your God-given gifts and should be celebrated. Practice celebrating and further discovering every day how your talents serve others and your purpose.

College degrees and the ability to read the *Wall Street Journal* without falling asleep should not be the only requirements to work in the business and financial sector. Your unique talents can be used to separate yourself from every other person with a resume.

Let's face it, on paper we can all look similar. How would your resume look using your secret sauce? What is it that makes you different? What defines you at your core? Your natural uniqueness should ooze from your pores. Discover your passions and natural talents and determine if you're living congruently through them.

Evaluate your current life conditions. If you are not using your God given talents everyday then most likely you're feeling stuck and repressed. If you are funny, then get on stage and be funny. If you are good at telling stories, then write stories or teach others how become a good story teller. By the way, I could use help with that!

The point is, use what comes naturally to you. That's the secret to living authentically happy. You will wake up every morning determined, with more passion and drive.

If you're having trouble discovering your passions, think about and evaluate what you do that is effortless. What makes you happy and serves others? Here are some questions to start opening your mind to your strengths and talents.

1. What did you dream of becoming as a child?
2. What are your natural abilities? What comes easy for you?
3. What would inspire and motivate you to get out of bed each day?
4. What are the most rewarding moments of your life? What talents did you use then?
5. What are you most effective at?
6. Where do you have the most impact?
7. The majority of books in your collection have what common theme?
8. What are 5 of your key strengths?
9. What are 5 things you're passionate about?
10. What do your friends seek your expertise on?
11. What is something unique that others may not know about you?
12. What would you do knowing that you couldn't fail?

It is important to recognize your passions to find your true purpose in life and equally important to use your passions as resources to stay in alignment with your authentic self. The key to fulfillment is living through your passions and purpose.

My formula for your success is:

$$Purpose + Passion = Fulfillment$$

In summary, connecting with your desires and passions will lead to your intention and deed to serve yourself and others. Your passions serve as the foundation blocks for living your purpose. Your authentic self awaits you to surrender into your passions so that it can navigate your life.

STEP 4: LET IT GO

Step Into Your Freedom

Inspired Insight:
"God has given us the opportunity to experience passion outside our comfort zone. If you let go then you can step into your greatest potential."
~ *Coach Delina*

WE ARE ALL different expressions of God and still all a part of the same oneness. We are unique as individuals but our essence is all the same and is beyond our physical body- this is oneness.

They say that you can find your true essence in the gap between your thoughts. For some people that gap can be an eternity. It might be easier to find your true essence by connecting with your heart.

Oneness is created by the expression of our true essence and the strongest force in the universe is *love*. I imagine that oneness looks like a web of white light connecting us all with insertion points into our hearts.

As individuals, we all have identity tags. These tags are our badges that we use to identity ourselves. An identity tag is my term for an inherited (surname or a family name) or chosen (married) name, a parental role or a professional title.

We use identity tags when introducing ourselves to others. Using an identity tag makes it easier to mentally group, sort, and process information because we associate familiarity with identity. Sometimes we place ourselves on a social evaluation scale when introduced to people who have identity tags such as doctor, esquire, Rabbi or Count of Monte Cristo.

Identifying ourselves with our identity tags is a great way to associate within a group and provides us with certainty of who we are in relation to others. Or does it?

How do you describe yourself? What are your identity tags? Complete this sentence, I am…

1. I am _____

2. I am _____

3. I am _____

4. I am _____

5. I am _____

6. I am _____

7. I am _____

8. I am _____

Great, now I want you to cross out #1 and #8 off the list. How do feel if we eliminate those? Do you feel a little confused? Did you feel resistant or hesitant to do it? Do you feel that eliminating those two strip away part of your identity? As if a part of who you are has been eliminated?

Now put a big X through your entire list- eliminating all of it. What are you left with? Do you feel raw? Naked? Powerless? Vulnerable? Freedom?

And although it feels different, are you still you?

This exercise is to give you the awareness that without your identity tags you still have the core essence of who you really are- authentic you.

If you strip away all of your titles and roles that you play and you stare at yourself in the mirror, who do you see? What is your core essence? What do you feel? Naked and raw without the titles or the roles, who are you?

At my bare bones, raw and stripped of all my titles and roles... I am *love*.

Identity tags are the roles we play but are not who we really are. Society has taught us to become attached to the roles that we play but the essence of who we really are has nothing to do with those roles. Our true essence is stronger than all of the titles and roles combined. Once you have found your core essence, then you no longer need to hold onto identity tags, especially the identities that have negative self-talk. Most of the time we hold onto self-sabotaging identities to protect us. Once you have found your core essence and who you really are then you need to show up that way. No longer put an identity mask over your face. How do you need to show up in order to live every day in your core essence?

We are a society of doers. In our society we are taught to go to school, get a degree and go to work. As we do and achieve, we attach to the titles and roles that are associated with that success. We connect so deeply with these identity tags that we create the illusion that this is who we really are. Soon you become "Doctor James Smith" instead of just Jim. Your identity tag is what changed you from Jim to Doctor James Smith, doctor is what you do it's not who you are. Not to detract from the honors that one should receive for achievement, however don't forget to remain the person at your core.

Remembering who you are without your identity tags prevents you from experiencing pain if at some point your roles disappear or become insignificant. Identity loss is a cause of severe emotional pain and suffering for many people. They feel lost when their title or role is taken away or no longer significant.

Furthermore, untreated emotional pain will manifest in the physical body. I have worked as a physician assistant for the past 15 years and I have treated lots of physical pain and emotional crisis working in various specialties of medicine.

My experience has been, especially in the Emergency Room, that most physical pain experienced is not associated with a pathological problem. Unfortunately Western medicine treats the symptoms but not the fundamental problem. I believe that most physical pain is secondary to unhealed and unresolved emotional stress and pain. Suicidal thoughts and attempts can also result from the endured suffering of identity loss.

I can remember a time when I struggled with my identity. I felt lost, angry and became argumentative. And I was frustrated with how I was "reacting" and not responding appropriately. This *reaction* coming from someone whose core essence is *love* was not congruent with my true values and beliefs.

The message here is to let go of the idea that your identity tags are who you really are. Attachment creates suffering. It is important to remember that your titles are earned, through hard work and achievement but that's what they are, achievements. When you become a doctor, lawyer, mechanic, or other tag, they in the end are occupations or roles that you fill but should not be who you are. Be proud but still be *you*. Learn how to *just be*. There is tremendous freedom that you can experience by giving yourself permission to *just be*. Imagine how refreshing and rewarding life could be if we could *just be* and not compete with self or others.

We are taught in our society that competition is associated with success. We will do whatever it takes to win or to be right. We are accustomed to creating separation by identifying winners and losers. The competition creates the belief that one needs to stand out above the rest to be significant.

This belief creates an urgency to be seen, to be the best and to finish first. What do you call a doctor who graduates last in his class? *Doctor!* Soon enough we are focusing all of our thoughts and actions for achieving significance – living through our Ego.

Let go of your Ego.

Our Ego is our enemy. It wants to keep you conditioned with the belief that you are driven to compete and to do whatever it takes to be more and have more. This shows up with desires for bigger and better material things. Cars, clothes, watches that we want yet don't need, maybe can't even afford but we feel it defines us by status and success.

This mindset is closely associated and holds the same energetic vibration of scarcity. Your Ego wants to keep you conditioned to believe that there isn't enough abundance to go around. It keeps you living within a mindset of scarcity so that you struggle for success and significance. Ego thrives on being significant. This mindset makes it difficult to obtain abundance.

Through Ego, you start to see the success of others as a threat and develop resentment. Instead of feeling grateful for what you have accomplished you may feel jealous of the accomplishments of others and tend to use that as a barometer for your own success. This creates further separation and frustration and pulls you away from your true identity and natural flow of the universe.

Imagine your Ego driven success as a triangle. When Ego kicks in and you try to compete and attain, you travel to the top of the triangle by separating yourself from others; you've attained and gotten to the top but found loneliness there too.

Your authentic and higher self does not need to compete to win. It doesn't struggle, sacrifice or worry. It operates with ease and flow. It perceives the world as an abundant place for all to be successful and happy. It focuses attention on obtaining fulfillment, love, compassion, gratitude and appreciation. If you focus on being happy and how you need to show up to feel happiness… then game over, you win!

If you can let go of your attachment to titles, roles, status, and significance through cars, jewelry, clothes and money- you will experience freedom. Let it go!

Subconsciously we live our lives seeking to gain the love and approval from others - especially from those whose love we craved the most as a child. We therefore carry the beliefs about our identity and character that have been told to us by others. These beliefs influence our perceptions and decisions. Since our decisions shape our destiny, it might be time to run your own race. Happiness cannot be found if you're living for the approval of others.

Let go of running someone else's race.

If you want to find your life's purpose then you need to let go of the expectations, beliefs, patterns, habits, fears and resistance that prevent you from running your own race.

When you let go of running someone else's race, you are letting go of their expectations, beliefs, fears and habits as your own. This results in gaining the clarity of your destined path so that you can start making decisions based on what you want and need to make you happy as opposed to what others define as happiness and success for you.

This "someone else" could be your parent, significant other, mentor, or friend. It is anyone other than yourself that you seek approval from. Picture their expectations, beliefs, patterns and fears as weights and then stack them with the amount of years that you have been carrying them around. That's the baggage you carry around daily. Does that feel heavy? Tiresome? Are you ready to let it go? How much longer do you want to carry around the baggage? What has it cost you in your life so far? Who has it hurt? What is missing in your life because of your baggage? What do you want in your life instead?

Letting go of running someone else's race gives you the freedom to experience the life that you were born to live. It is your birthright to live out your dreams and passions. You cannot attract new opportunities and design the life of your dreams unless you let go of the patterns that prevent. Let go of the expectations, old beliefs, patterns of self-sabotage, fears, and resistance. Liberate yourself from the heavy baggage. It's not yours unless you want to continue holding onto it. It doesn't serve you moving forward. Let it go and experience freedom! Create the space for abundance and opportunity to enter into your life.

Don't live someone else's dream, listen to your heart and live your dream. Don't let others tell you what to do or how to create your destiny.

If I had evaluated how I wanted to feel in my career, I would've realized that I valued creativity, inspiration, and passion. That would've led me down a very different path. There were clues along the way but I wasn't willing to let it go.

Let go of the comfort zone

Sometimes we get too comfortable. Living with purpose and passion requires you at times to live outside of your comfort zone. Staying in your comfort zone actually prevents you from expanding and experiencing your greatness.

"Life begins at the end of your comfort zone."

Stepping outside of your comfort zone will give you the opportunity to create a better experience for yourself. You will experience vitality, motivation and passion. I challenge you to let go of that which is comfortable for you. Consider the things that keep you comfortable and decide right now which of these things are actually preventing you from living fully and completely to your fullest potential.

Have you been playing small? Have you been staying in your comfort zone?

Let go of the pacifier and step outside of your comfort zone.

In order to comfortably stretch outside the comfort zone and grow, we need to manage – or eliminate – any subconscious stress and anxiety that we've associated with change. You must find that zone edge and embrace it instead of succumbing to your fears. Staying in your comfort zone will not serve you well long term. In fact, it can feel like purgatory. When you hesitate to expand and evolve you may feel that you're living a life sentence instead of living life.

Passion is found outside of your comfort zone. The more you practice living outside your comfort zone, the more authentic and fully present you will be in life.

Let go of idea that achievement equals fulfillment.

For many, there is a belief that success requires hard work, long hours, struggle, discipline and sacrifice. We are raised to believe that life is a struggle. "No pain, no gain." We struggle for power, approval and appreciation.

We believe that the harder we work, the more we become, and the bigger the reward. This belief about success causes us to work extended hours and sacrifice our well-being and time. The longer we sacrifice and neglect ourselves, the more it becomes expected and a baseline for our new "normal."

Eventually, we become drained, exhausted and disconnected. We function daily feeling disengaged and numb. We no longer enjoy activities that once brought us joy. This leads to depression, anxiety, and frustration, overwhelm and stress. This leads to a void in your life that wants to be filled. At that point, it's not uncommon for us to replenish ourselves with love, nurturance and connection through alcohol, food, gambling, sex, shopping or anti-depressants.

Success without fulfillment feels like failure.

It is our responsibility to let go of our twisted, engrained beliefs regarding success and fulfillment. Letting go of the idea that accumulated achievements equals success and fulfillment will help you to experience freedom and happiness.

What if success meant learning, experiencing, and growing instead of achievement. A goal is great to have but if achieving the goal is your only measurement for success then you will feel failure in the form of un-fulfillment.

Instead of measuring success by your achievements try using a measurement that is connected to your passions. Personal growth, for example, became my measurement for success. So now anytime I invest in my personal growth I feel successful without needing a diploma or certificate. Plus now I feel the fulfillment of success along the way. The goal is to celebrate along the journey, not just at the finish line.

If you're only looking at success as the finish line, then you're missing the opportunity to have fun along the way. The finish line doesn't give you lasting fulfillment. It is a snap shot euphoric moment of time.

The journey, experience, and your transformation along the way gives you the fulfillment, and should be your measurement of success. Set yourself up to win and celebrate every day.

My story

My parents divorced when I was still a baby. My mother remained in good relations with the Fajardo family and so I would visit regularly to see my father, grandparents and cousins. It was uncomfortable for me to see my father because he felt "alien" to me. Trust was never built in that relationship as a child. I was not verbally or sexually abused, but is there such a thing as nonverbal abuse? It felt like avoidance abuse. He would sit in stillness and stare at me but not talk or try to connect. It was weird. But the dynamics with my paternal side of the family otherwise was very healthy, loving and inviting. I realize now that at that time, my father had his own issues and was unable to cope with being a father. We have a healthier relationship now, he always wants to talk and connect- in fact, he can't stop talking. It is ironic, not being raised by my father, that we are more alike than I am with my mother.

My mother and I lived with maternal grandparents - a modest home that my grandfather built in Long Island, NY. I was raised watching my mother stress and struggle financially. She sometimes worked 2-3 jobs to make ends meet.

I didn't have my own bedroom until we moved to Florida at around age 11 or 12. Yes that means that I either slept in the same bedroom as my mother or my room was converted from some "other room."

I remember being so excited about having my own space. It felt so cool having my own bedroom and bathroom, but that was until I saw my friends' homes.

To give you a more insight, we had a small 2Bed/2Bath condo in Coral Springs, Florida; an environment similar to living in Boca Raton at the time. If you know Boca then you understand. It was a very affluent, upscale environment. The residents all very successful, working professionals that drove luxury vehicles and wore designer clothing. Everything was about status. My high school student parking lot had nicer cars than the employee lot. It was not uncommon to see students drive up in their new BMW's, Mercedes Benz, Jeep Wranglers, loaded trucks etc.

My first car was a new red Mazda 323 GTX, which I paid for by working a telemarketing job after school; where my sleazy boss slapped my ass every time he walked by. This was stacking on my already conflicting and confusing beliefs about men. It didn't help my trust issues from childhood.

It was a blessing that I was well liked and had many friends in school. I was exposed to their lifestyles and which made me feel normal. The contrast was that I was living in a small condo and yet visiting my friends that lived in private estates - where an attendant would buzz me through a private gate. Their homes were mansions to me; game rooms, bathrooms bigger than my bedroom, huge heated pools, hot tubs, golf courses in their backyard. Living with that daily contrast planted the seeds of growth that developed my beliefs around success.

As a college student, I had big aspirations for a career and future but I was confused about my direction. I was always ambitious and considered an overachiever. I had the belief that achievements would bring fulfillment and happiness. I equated success with status, money and professions such as doctor, lawyer, and traders in the stock market.

My belief was:
success = money = status = being a professional

I had expectations from all over: family, friends, guidance counselors, mentors, society, colleagues, and most importantly myself. The combination of my beliefs, expectations and fears created inner conflict and a competitive nature within. I began to strive and achieve not for myself, but for the status and the image that my expectations created.

I spent well over $100,000 in school loans for an identity tag.

My passions and interests were ignored because they were effortless, not requiring "hard work." They were considered hobbies and not a "real profession." I strived to live up to my expectations. I didn't let go of running someone else's race.

My compelling vision of success included status, money and achievements. I never considered happiness, fulfillment, or passion. I thought the graduate degree hung on the wall would be more important than the passion within my heart.

I assumed the money and success from my achievements would provide the happiness and stability that I sought. I never considered that the finish line might not deliver fulfillment.

After completing my graduate studies I was enthusiastic about my future and motivated by my first "real" paycheck. With the money I was able to afford my lifestyle- my own apartment in Hoboken, NJ, a new car, new clothes, summer share houses in the Hamptons, and late night partying in NYC. I kept myself distracted with my social and professional life: friends, ski trips, dinners, boyfriends and work. My lifestyle was very fast-paced and filled with variety and excitement.

Early into my career, I became disappointed and frustrated with medicine and how operational it was. I was disappointed by how robotic I had become- jaded and numb. I was efficient at treating my patients and their symptoms but unfulfilled by my efforts.

At that time I was doing open-heart surgery and saving lives in the operating room. I was a first assistant surgeon in Cardio-Thoracic surgery in my early 20's. I guess this is the equivalent to working on Wall Street at the same age while managing millions of dollars daily for people triple your age. It was the high life and loaded with stress. Twice to three times daily, I was opening thoracic chests, sewing on beating hearts, harvesting veins and arteries, managing my stress plus the surgeon and consulting with cardiologists, interventionists and patient's families. I was exhausted plus unfulfilled.

After working 70-80 hours a week I always needed a weekend of exploding fun. The wear and tear on my body didn't feel good but the six figure salary in my early 20's sufficed. With my early beliefs, irresponsible spending habits, and self-sabotaging patterns there was no way I was leaving. I was the poster child for *my* definition of success. I could walk outside my front door and have access to4 dry cleaners, 12 restaurants, 10 bars, 3 nail salons, Starbucks and a Dunkin Donuts on my block. God bless Hoboken. What else could I possibly need? The parking was always a problem, but I managed.

I had everything I needed to be happy… or did I?

Everything was convenient except I lacked the passion and connection with self and others. I had an insatiable thirst to do and be something different. I was mostly frustrated with my expectations and the false illusion that finishing school, having status, and being a professional would bring me happiness, freedom and fulfillment. The truth was that I was unhappy, stuck and a slave to my workplace.

The career eventually drained my vitality. I compensated with food to nurture myself. Fifteen years later I realized that I had exited Highway Purpose a long time ago and I needed to find my *u-turn*. I just wanted to be free and happy. I remember one day flipping through a magazine and admiring a picture that represented the freedom that I wanted to feel. That picture later became the icon of my compelling vision. It reminded me of how I wanted to feel everyday. Except,

I needed to let go of my pacifier and step outside my comfort zone.

I wouldn't say it occurred a few years too late, I would say it was right on schedule. Had I not gone through life as I did, then I wouldn't have the life lessons to share my message with you. I would be speaking on theory rather than life experience. I prefer to speak from experience.

I learned my lessons the hard way but you don't have to. Allow my journey to awaken you and give you the insights that you need to make the best decisions for your life. Take my advice and *Let it Go!*

Now I ask you, what do you need to let go?

Do you feel that you need to "work hard" and struggle in life in order to feel successful?

Is success defined and measured by your achievements and accomplished tasks?

Are you willing to change your measurement for success and fulfillment?

In the past, what had to happen in order for you to feel successful?

_____

_____

_____

_____

What are you willing to believe about success moving forward?

_____

_____

_____

_____

What titles and roles do you need to detach from? This means liberating yourself from the idea that those titles or roles are who you really are:

1. _____

2. _____

3. _____

4. _____

5. _____

What do you need to let go of to step outside your comfort zone?

_____

_____

Whose love did you crave the most growing up as a child?

_____

Who do you need to let go living the approval of?

_____

Are you willing to let go of the expectations, rules, fears and beliefs that prevent you from achieving real happiness?

What beliefs, self-sabotaging patterns, or fears do you need to let go of?

_____

_____

_____

_____

In summary, your past experiences have given you everything that you need to move towards living with purpose.

If you want to live with purpose, you must be willing to let some things go.

Each step moving towards your purpose will lead to your additional strength and courage. And the passion, happiness and fulfillment experienced along the way will give you the motivation and drive to continue the journey. Holding onto what prevents this growth will stifle your authentic identity and core essence. *You must be willing to let it go!*

Let go with the intentions to embrace and explore your true purpose. As you let go, you will open up to possibility and your destiny. Give yourself free reign to stretch yourself beyond your comfort zone. Life is a journey. Keep your eye on your compelling vision and enjoy the journey but most importantly, run your own race.

STEP 5: FOCUS ON WHAT YOU WANT

Clarity is Power

Inspired Insight:
"Learn to harness the power of intention with your goals and this will bring you everything you desire." ~ Coach Delina

ONE OF THE MOST IMPORTANT STEPS in finding your true purpose in life is focusing on what you want. Clarity is power and needed to declare your outcome. Without clarity on what you really want, your achievements become a mixed result of the confusion that you carry along the way.

A journey with an unknown destination is just another way to say you are lost.

This chapter centers on developing a compelling vision and focusing on what you want. This step is vital because ambivalent feelings about your destination can slow you down and deter you, but increasing your attention to what you want accelerates your manifestation process. It's time to develop your compelling vision!

Your compelling vision can be considered your destination point. It would be difficult to arrive at a location if you didn't know what your destination was. This is equally true if you go through life without direction, wasting your time and energy.

Clarity on your destination- your compelling vision- gets you to the destination. It's important to note that your journey to the destination can detour so don't get attached to a single destination path. Just remain clear on what you want and to stay the course, focused on that intention with passion and dedication. Having clarity gives you the ability to deflect distractions instead of letting them become a hindrance.

Every thought, belief, and decision creates your reality. They affect your journey and course towards your destination. You can either create multiple pot holes or a smooth ride on your journey with your thoughts, beliefs and decisions. Which would you prefer? Hitting a pot hole on I-95 at 65 miles per hour in a small Honda hurts!

Let's consider your thoughts, beliefs and decisions as rest stops or exits on a highway - *Highway Purpose*. If you're gaining momentum along Highway Purpose towards your destination and you get a negative thought or belief, you can either make a bad decision based on that belief and exit the highway, or you can pause with awareness at the rest stop and hit the reset button, regain your focus, eliminate bodily fluids and refuel.

Can you see the difference? The good news about exiting the highway is that there is always a place to make a u-turn.

Another thing to anticipate on your journey down Highway Purpose are detour signs. Detours can be a good thing. They are different from exits because they still lead you in the direction towards your purpose. You still gain momentum in the right direction on a detour.

The purpose of the flagman in the bright orange vest waving you onto unknown streets may throw you off at first, making you feel unsure and hesitant because of the unknown path that lies ahead. But the purpose is to detour you away from unsafe or unprepared territory. However, taking another road that will lead to your same destination.

Detours are not meant to prevent you but merely steer you in a direction that will strengthen your character and skills to prepare you for the arrival of your destination. Every detour has a purpose to serve you. Detours are part of God's plan and he promises to get you to your final destination.

Stay flexible on your journey towards finding your true purpose. The journey requires you to detach from a single outcome and the path in getting there from your perspective.

Think of your flexibility as your GPS navigation. The shortest distance between two places is a straight line, but a straight line is not the only way to cover the distance between two places. Stay open and allow the universe to take care of the details, it has a much grander plan for your purpose. You can even go as far as anticipating and considering other ways to get to your destination beforehand.

Once you start this path by getting clarity on your purpose, stay detached of how to serve that purpose and remain flexible on how you arrive at your purpose. If you're attached and rigid in your ways, then you'll miss the abundance of possibilities that are available to you.

Of equal importance, do not get caught up in the idea that there is only 1 single life purpose for you to live. New purposes are evolving every moment. There are multiple purposes for you to live in your lifetime. It's only an illusion that you need to find 1 single life purpose.

That illusion creates stress, frustration and overwhelm in trying to find "the big one." Instead, focus on finding what's in your heart in the present moment and that will always lead you towards a life of purpose.

More often than not, you will start identifying with a life's purpose that will lead you into a different purpose, path and destination. Your final destination can change over time. In fact, it may change multiple times. Your destination may start out as seeking purpose but may lead to more through your enlightenment and journey.

The more flexible you are, the more opportunity you have for realizing your deepest desires. Stay open, flexible and detached. The universe wants to deliver infinite opportunities for you to manifest your dreams. Sometimes your dreams expand or change once your journey towards your destination has begun, consider all new opportunities that may fulfill your purpose. Change is healthy and leads to vitality and passion.

Another thing to consider when contemplating change is that we outgrow our purposes. What might have served as your purpose in the past may no longer serve you currently. If you have expanded and grown through your purpose then it's time to get back on Highway Purpose towards your next destination- a higher purpose. If you have outgrown a purpose in this stage of your life, then you most likely are evolving into a stronger identity and a deeper meaning for your life.

Life is a ladder. Each destination is a step to launch your next journey. Along the way, you will grow and learn more about yourself and your passions. You will develop new desires and interests. New opportunities will be created. It is important to remain open-minded, flexible and mindful. This all allows for infinite possibility. Don't be frightened by your power beyond measure.

The key to manifesting your desires is to *solely* focus on what you want. A common mistake we make is that we simultaneously focus on what we want plus focus subconsciously on its contrast - what we don't want - out of fear.

There is a difference between awareness of contrast and being afraid of it. When we are fearful of something we can still attract into our experience. What we focus on we attract. Focusing on what you want and being fearful (hence focused) on what you don't want sends mixed signals to the universe and then simultaneously you experience a bit of both.

Knowing what you *don't* want is usually a result from experience or learning by example. Such as:

- Don't touch a hot stove,
- Don't go skiing without a helmet,
- Don't drive over the speed limit
- Don't poke a bear with a short stick

Acknowledging the contrast is only helpful to give you clarity on what you *do* want. The more attention and focus you give what you *don't* want, the more power you give it.

Whatever you put enough attention to will become your reality.

Your current life is partly a manifestation of what you focused on in the past. Yes some things are out of your control, but the things that are within your control, result from your prior thoughts. If you're in debt then you did not solely focus on abundance. You get what you put enough attention to.

Focusing on what you want and your compelling vision requires discipline and for you to monitor the thoughts of your conscious and subconscious mind. Just as it is important to be mindful of your thoughts, it is just as important to be aware of the words that deliver your message.

You should work to develop a heightened sensory acuity to your thoughts and language used moment-to-moment. Negativity and fear within the subconscious mind will affect your conscious thoughts, words and actions. Once you notice this happening, pause, breathe, and use a magic eraser to erase it from your brain.

The magic eraser doesn't work to erase voiced words, which may leave a scar and cause pain to yourself and others. Remember, your words have creative power. Be mindful of your focus and words because they manifest your future. Let your emotions be your indicator.

A great indicator to remind you to shift your attention and focus to what you want versus its contrast is your emotions. It is important to pay attention to your emotions because they give you the answers to whether you should pursue those thoughts or not. If your emotions aren't serving you then use the magic eraser and erase the associated thoughts with those emotions. Breathe, reset and start over!

Always check in with your emotions. If you feel alive, inspired, motivated, happy, or creative, then you're on Highway Purpose. By contrast, if you're feeling angry, fearful, exhausted, fatigued, depressed, anxious, frustrated, stressed or overwhelmed then somewhere you exited the highway and need to make a u-turn. What road are you currently on?

It was when I committed to focusing on how I wanted to feel moving forward and my compelling vision that I started manifesting happiness through my purpose. Focusing on my compelling vision kept me aligned with my mission. Living my compelling vision gives me freedom and fulfillment that I seek. This is what I wish for you.

Only you have the power to create the experience and emotions that you want to feel daily. How do you want to show up today?

It's now your turn to imagine and create your destiny. Here is your opportunity to focus on what you want and develop your compelling vision!

What do you REALLY want?

_____

_____

_____

_____

_____

_____

How do you want to feel moving forward in your life?

_____

_____

_____

What do you want to accomplish, create, or give?

_____

_____

_____

What is most important to you in life?

_____

_____

_____

What is your ultimate goal?

_____

_____

_____

What are you committed to achieving?

_____

_____

_____

What are you willing to fight for?

_____

_____

_____

In summary, I am willing to fight for life's purpose. I believe that you should be living your purpose daily. Alignment and congruency with your identity starts the journey. Focusing on your compelling vision sets the destination. Now it's time to step into your freedom.

STEP 6: SPEAK YOUR TRUTH

Discover Your Authentic Voice

Inspired Insight:
"How you show up for yourself and others makes a difference." ~
Coach Delina

Find Personal Power In Speaking Your Truth

THERE IS A POWERFUL CONNECTION between speaking your truth and living your purpose. This chapter will teach you how to connect with your personal power through speaking your truth. When speaking your truth, ask yourself:

- Am I owning my identity with certainty? Am I speaking my truth? If not, why not?

- Is fear keeping me from speaking my truth?

- Who do I need to be?

- How do I need to show up?

You must come from a place of authenticity to speak your truth. When you learn to speak from your authentic self – your truth – you'll find yourself in a place of integrity, freedom, and peace.

Always remember:

You must speak your truth, acknowledging who you truly are, as your authentic self, in order to sustain your purpose.

You must trust your purpose because once you start speaking your truth you are always sharing purpose.

And if you want to be authentically influential in the eyes of others, you must always come from a place of truth.

Speaking truth comes easier for some than for others. If this is something you are not easily comfortable with then approach this chapter with the intention to learn to trust your voice and become courageous. Most importantly, you must know what your truth is for yourself first. Then you must live your truth and walk your talk. Until you learn do this, you won't be able to authentically speak your truth with others.

What is Your Real Truth?

What does the statement, "And the truth shall set you free," mean to you? The truth will indeed set you free, but first you must know what your real truth is.

You may think that you are speaking from your truth every day, but it's possible that you've taken your real truth and buried it under layers of lies, added in some drama and spice, and that once it was spoken and welcomed by a captive audience, it became a pseudo-truth. It's easy to substitute your real truth with a pseudo-truth.

It's easy to forget what is really true after creating so many pseudo-truths. We tell ourselves:

My Story + Good Response=Truth

We also think speaking a pseudo-truth aloud will somehow protect from others seeing our imperfections and weaknesses. We live in a world where so-called "reality" media has a huge following and demand. It generates billions of dollars in revenue off of characters that are supposed to be true people, but instead they are manufactured to fit the needs an audience. At times do you see yourself doing the same?

Say Hello to Your Authentic Self

It can be painful to live in reality, taking off the social shield, your manufactured truth, but you can do it. The irony is that the reward from taking off your social shield is what you seek from wearing it- confidence and certainty.

I'm sure you remember a time when you have spoken up for something you strongly believed in. What made you do that? Who did you become? How did you show up? How did it feel afterwards?

You probably felt courageous and confident because your truth was valuable and served others. Your authentic truth serves as a way to communicate your message, mission and purpose in life.

Your core values, beliefs, and their associated meanings have all been accumulated from past experiences. In order to speak your truth you need to know what truth resonates within you first.

What is Your Authentic Truth?

• Who am I?

• Why was I created?

• What is my purpose?

• What truth resonates about my purpose?

• What is most important to me?

Remember, speaking your truth is about knowing and expressing who you really are, and embracing that identity with 100% certainty. Speaking your truth is your opportunity to share with others who you really are, your core beliefs and values. To speak your truth, you must be honest with yourself.

Ask yourself:

1.   What do I believe in so strongly that the opposite would be a deal breaker for me?

2.   What values and rules if violated would cause me to detach and remove myself from a situation?

3.   What lasting impression do I want to leave?

What – at your core – is important to you? What beliefs are near and dear to your heart; the things that get you fired-up to talk about? What are you passionate talking about? Discover the answers for yourself first. Make sure they spark something within. Once you're certain of your truth for yourself then start expressing and sharing those points of view with others.

Most feel comfortable voicing programmed responses - a.k.a. small talk, but uncomfortable voicing their passions, core beliefs, and values – a.k.a. their truth. Don't you get tired of the same old small talk?

What is your name? What do you do? Where do you live? How old are you?

Do you really care?

How about starting a conversation with,
"What are your passions? What motivates you? What was the most embarrassing thing that ever happened to you? What do you hate? What do you love?"

I think these questions generate a much more interesting conversation. At the very least you will both laugh from sharing an embarrassing moment. Hopefully you will trust that speaking your truth is safe and fun. Be willing to consider it.

The Reasons Why

If you're wondering why you should consider speaking your truth at all, then consider the following:

Have you been influenced by this book so far? Have you made distinctions that would empower you moving forward? Do you feel inspired?

That's a result of me speaking my truth!

Have you ever been influenced by someone you know-maybe they said something that changed your life?

That was a result of them speaking their truth!

Have you ever been inspired, encouraged or moved by a complete stranger because you resonated with their honesty and authenticity in their words?

That was a result of them speaking their truth!

So when considering not speaking your truth, please also consider how many people you are robbing from your influence, insights, wisdom, creativity, inspiration, and encouragement.

Speaking your truth is not just about liberating yourself, it's also a way for you to serve your purpose by communicating your message.

Whether you're aware of it at the time or not, your truth always has a message for someone else. Everybody's truth, if authentic and from a servant's heart, has a purpose to serve others. Your truth is the answer and the breakthrough that someone else has been searching for, and needs.

Your truth is a way to make a difference. And your message can go viral. Imagine that you're pollinating many to grow and blossom with your message, starting with a single bee. If the garden metaphor isn't working, just know that your truth is bigger than you - it's about making a difference in this world using your authenticity.

~

Things to Consider

1. Practice Vulnerability

Are you ready to get vulnerable? It is important to step outside of your comfort zone and step into vulnerability. We frequently stop ourselves from speaking our truth because we fear vulnerability, but in reality, vulnerability is more powerful!

You will become more effective at speaking your truth if you practice vulnerability. Every time you show your vulnerable side, you are exercising more of your personal power. You must learn to trust your exposed, vulnerable self, and become comfortable letting your guard down and allowing your authenticity to shine, like diamonds in the sky.

Vulnerability takes practice, but just like anything else that's worth a good result, we need to condition the skill. I still work on being vulnerable. I'm not saying that it's easy, but it has a greater influence and impact on others.

Speaking from a place of vulnerability requires you to speak from your heart and not from your head. Speaking from your heart has a different tonality and pitch to your words.

Words from your heart space will resonate differently than words from a mental place. When you speak from your heart -a place of vulnerability – you can easily develop rapport with others. People are able to connect easily when your message is delivered from a place of truth and authenticity. The goal is to feel great, grounded, centered, calm, and confident while being vulnerable and speaking from your heart.

2. Fear is the Enemy

Fear is the enemy of your vulnerable self. Fear can be the biggest hindrance to vulnerability on the journey to speaking your truth. Sometimes just the thought of embarrassment or judgment being made against us is enough to keep us silent and hiding from our truth.

Fear is an evil that prevents us from progress.

Fear will prevent you from getting what you want in life and will stop you from speaking your truth if you allow it. It can cause you to self-sabotage and self-destruct. Fear is a foe that wants to be a friend.

In fact, fear even wants us to depend on it and invite it into situations and events that challenge us. Fear wants us to ignore that it's just an emotion and to forget that we have ultimate control over it.

Stop Inviting Fear to the Party

In order to easily speak your truth, stop inviting fear to your parties. Despite its toxicity, why do we continue to invite fear into our lives, hearts, and minds? Why do we give it full access to our "mission control center" of our existence, where it navigates our focus and decides for us?

Do you really want fear to control your decisions and destiny? Let's not friend fear. Don't give it permission into your mission control center.

Think about it this way, if fear had a Facebook page, would you 'Like' it? Would you want to see and associate with its friends on Facebook? Imagine what that page would look like. Its Facebook friends would all be similar toxic emotions: anger, insecurity, overwhelm, frustration, anxiety, depression, and so on.

Do you want to be friends with them, too? Remember the saying, "You are the company you keep!" I don't know about you, but I want my destiny shaped by my personal power, not by fear or any of its friends on Facebook. Here's a solution,

Put Fear to Work for You

Every experience has a lesson to teach, even the emotion of fear. Next time you find yourself dealing with fear on speaking your truth:

- Acknowledge and learn the possible lesson to be learned from that fear. Otherwise, the pattern will repeat.

- See fear for what it is – just an emotion.

- Acknowledge the voice of fear but then choose to listen to another inner voice instead – we have multiple advisors within. Perhaps your advisor named courage might like to speak up. Say to fear,
  Thank you fear for your warning. I hear and acknowledge you, but at this time I'm choosing to listen to courage instead! Thank you, but no thank you!

- Ask yourself, *Is my perception of this situation really true? Is the belief that I have adopted about this based on reality, or could it be perceived differently? How would someone that easily speaks their truth perceive this?*

- Ask yourself, *What are the other possibilities that this could be?* Most likely, the other possibilities will not elicit fear.

The goal is to condition your mind into substituting fear with a new and empowering meaning.

3. Own your truth

Once you've found your truth, believe in it and own it. If you can't believe in your own truth with 100% certainty then don't expect others to. You must have certainty and strength in your truth because others will challenge it. Don't become discouraged by their challenge, it's not intended to deflate you. Welcome its potential- an additional pillar of strength.

Your truth is a source of your personal power. You must resonate with it. It should support your essence and authentic identity; it should empower you.

No one can take away your truth or personal power unless you give permission.

Own your personal power and truth by acknowledging that you know what is best for you. Don't allow others to persuade you into their values and beliefs.

No matter how close a friend or average an acquaintance, no one knows your truth except you. Own it, speak it and be proud of it. Your truth will set you free!

4. Be Respectful of Truth

I cannot express how important it is to be respectful of others while they're speaking their truth. Being respectful means without judgment, resistance or being defensive.

It's important to understand that one's truth is their unique expression of their experience, and their experience has nothing to do with your own.

Even if you are a part of their story, what they feel and their opinion of the story remains their experience of it. To take their truth personally and react to it with judgment or defensiveness would be a disservice to them. It's important not to become defensive. Just be present.

Remember, it's not about you; it's about their experience. Allowing others to heal through their own expressions of truth is a great gift to give. In return, they will respond with relief, appreciation, and love.

Instead of taking it personally, try allowing them to speak their truth without taking responsibility for anything they may say. Be present and listen, understanding that it has nothing to do with you, and everything to do with their experience. Give others your full attention in their moment of truth without placing judgment on them or putting resistance in their way.

Resistance and judgment are strong, negative, and nonverbal vibrations that are easily transferred via body language, lack of attention and a lack of presence. This includes shaking your head, texting, using the phone, rolling your eyes, interrupting, or just focusing on something else while they speak.

Those attitudes can make others feel uncomfortable, insecure, fearful, stupid, and silly. Those emotions can lead to a person's fear of speaking their truth in the future, further limiting and preventing them from living in their personal power. Show them the respect that you would like in return.

5. Children Should be Heard

If you want your children to learn how to comfortably speak their truth as an adult then be present and listen to them now.

When was the last time you really wanted to say something but didn't because you thought it wouldn't matter?

Have you considered the possibility that those beliefs were created from your childhood? Make everything a child says count and matter. The same restrictions from speaking your truth as a child could be discouraging you from speaking it today.

I can recall being disciplined for speaking aloud as far back as elementary school, but now I can see that what I was actually being told was that speaking my truth was inappropriate. At the time, my truth was very different from what it is now, though nonetheless, it was valid to me. My teacher, should have just listened . . . Cinderella needed her glass slipper and I had it in my backpack!

We are trained at a young age to be quiet. As children without positive reinforcement and encouragement to express ourselves, how can we then recognize our voice as adults. It's fascinating to me that as children, we are reprimanded if we speak-up, but later on, as adults, we are expected to step up and speak up on a regular basis. No wonder there are so many phobias related to public speaking. There is a paradox between our being raised to be quiet and obedient, and how we are expected to behave as adults – outgoing and dynamic presenters. It might be helpful to encourage speaking our truth at an early age.

6. Practice Speaking Your Truth –

Truth Exercise:

Knowing your truth and speaking it freely is extremely empowering. Here is what I call my "word vomit" exercise to practice speaking your truth. The rules are:

1. Speak out loud,
2. Do not filter your words,
3. Do not judge yourself for what is being said
4. Give yourself permission to word vomit
5. Keep repeating the phrase followed by a **different** truth until you feel relaxed and liberated

Say to yourself out loud:

"The truth is_____

and the truth is _____."

The Truth Will Set You Free

Every day that you fail to speak and live your truth, you limit your potential to feel passion. Here are some checkpoints you can follow to help you stay in your truth:

- Continue to be honest with yourself and acknowledge your truth to yourself and others.

- Don't allow another person's perception to influence your truth.

- Give yourself permission to express yourself.

- Remember that your truth liberates you but also serves by empowering others.

- Remember that vulnerability is power!

STEP 7: USE YOUR RESOURCES

Everything You Need Is Within You Now

Inspired Insight:

"The enemy in your own mind always fights the hardest when you are closest to your success."~ *Coach Delina*

HAVE YOU EVER NOTICED the closer you get to success something inevitably happens to try and sabotage your efforts? I can remember my computer crashing *twice* just before a deadline, and after everything was 90% done. This most recently happened to me today, just before writing this chapter. My computer crashed with a virus from an application I downloaded to access a font for my campaign - *got purpose?*

Did I mention that *I downloaded it?* I couldn't even pawn off the blame onto someone else. Yes this is sad but true. I wasted time trying to upload a font and as a result, I uploaded an application that crashed my computer, with two chapters left to write.

As I realized what happened, all the thoughts that raced through my head were not pleasant or from a space of love or gratitude. In fact, it was more the opposite: worry, stress, overwhelm, self-inflicted anger, and blame. Ok, enough of the niceties, I wanted blood!

However even as anger was my first emotion in this situation there had to be a reason for my stupidity and temporary lack of good judgment. I had to blame something other than myself and since nobody else was around, I went right to the source. Was the universe testing me? I started imagining it saying, "Are you really going to own this stuff or just preach it?"

I reminded myself to practice what I preach, to find the gift in the lesson, and to evolve from it. Has anything similar happened to you? If you're wondering what happened next, well let's just say that I was extremely grateful for my aligned identity and sane judgment with my prior investment in Apple Care Protection Plan.

There are many variables that affect our response to challenges. What if you discovered that you already have the resources of strength within to overcome challenges in advance? Would you use them?

You know, there is a difference between resources and resourcefulness. *Resourcefulness* means you are actually using your resources that are available to you. Many people think they don't have enough resources, when in fact, there is an abundance of resources; just not enough resourcefulness. So I ask again, if you discovered that you have the resources of strength within to overcome any challenge or obstacle, would you use them?

I believe that we have many powerful resources within that can prepare us for any challenging encounter, but my top three are:

1. Emotions
2. Beliefs
3. Values

The experiences in your lifetime have made these resources uniquely powerful to you. If you reflect on times in your life where you have been challenged but succeeded, I'm sure you can clearly pinpoint what it was that made you endure.

In the same fashion, during times of failure, after honest reflection, you also know why you didn't rise to the occasion. In this chapter, you will reveal your current mindset and determine if it's helping you fulfill your goals or not. We will re-create and strengthen your resources so that you can use them as assets moving forward.

On a recent trip to my stomping grounds, New York City, I found myself visiting the Intrepid Sea Air and Space Museum with my friend John McCue. We needed a little writing inspiration so we decided to see one of the West Side's largest attractions (Or rather, my car was being serviced on 57th and 12th Avenue and this was within walking distance... either way go with it, please!)

One of the largest and key exhibits there was the former U.S.S. Growler Missile Submarine, constructed in 1954 and launched and commissioned in 1958. The semi-guided tour gives you an up-close and personal look at the life of the 87 crewmembers that were aboard this vessel during World War II.

Now mind you I have conquered many fears in my life, fear of change, fear of the unknown, even a fear of *clowns*. But there was another fear I would need to confront that rarely shows its little head. Upon entering the exhibit I was quickly reminded that I have a terrible fear of small, enclosed spaces – I am claustrophobic!

While looking at this massive hulk sitting atop the water, with an overall length of 322 feet and a width of 30 feet, you wouldn't think the small tight space would be a problem. Deciding to endure I figured, "I got this."

Keeping my fear to myself, I decided to keep my horror of enclosed spaces to myself, leap outside of my comfort zone and together we paid the $64 entrance fee to step into a cold-war era nuclear submarine. We even took a, now ironic, picture of us entering the boat with excited, jovial faces. I had no idea what would challenge us ahead.

Within 15 feet of entering the first passageway on the boat I realized that I had made a huge mistake but we couldn't turn back. Adding fuel to the fire, John, my supposed rock to help me get through this, decided this was a great time to tell me that he was about to shit himself because he too is highly claustrophobic!

REALLY?

The average passageway onboard is approximately 2.5 feet wide. John's shoulders touched both sides of the narrow enclosure.

Picture feeling imprisoned in the very first passageway, the size of which you can't quite stand up in and not enough space to turn around in since we are packed in like sardines. Some of the immediate physical reactions to this standstill included:

- Heart palpitations, heart beating a mile a minute.
- Palms sweating and throat completely dry. The water they confiscated while entering the museum would have come in handy.
- You start looking around impatiently to try and see what the holdup is, if there is an avenue of escape or any other optical body you can focus on to help ease the anxiety you are now feeling.
- You start to unfairly decide that this was definitely your friend's idea and you begin planning the penalty phase of their trial in your head.

Just as I am having irrational thoughts and sheer panic is about to set in, I discover the cause of this unforeseen logjam. There were five senior citizens who couldn't figure out how to maneuver through the first access hatch in the bow of the boat.

Are you kidding me? It's a hole! Go through it!

To endure such terror in the supposed name of education and entertainment, I had to find something to help ease the fear and increase my confidence so I could progress forward as planned. I needed to overcome this because turning around was physically impossible. We were packed in like sardines.

My friend began quietly muttering humorous quips about the rise in his body temperature, our inability to turn around and the overall irony of the situation we put ourselves in. I began laughing and found that the more insane, absurd and exaggerated the humor was, the more I laughed, and the less I thought about the proceeding panic.

As I contributed to the stand-up act already in progress, I felt my mind switch from fear and worry to ease and calm. This reduced my anxiety and improved my comfort level greatly. Being stuck in such a small space, *laughter* was our method of finding the courage to remain present and calm and not have a panic attack.

Before I knew it, Aunt Betty and friends had made their way into the next compartment and we were moving. In our situation, we had found our *Sweet Spot* with laughter and made it our *Emotional Home*.

Your Emotional Home

What I learned from that experience is that we need to find our sweet spot and our emotional home. Challenges will occur during your quest to live your purpose. The enemy in your own mind always fights the hardest when you are closest to your success. How you filter your experience will determine how you feel your experience. Our filters are our "shades" that perceive everything. It's like the difference between looking through a lens that is rose tinted versus mud-splattered.

Your filters will perceive and unconsciously sort the information before you have an emotional reaction. They predetermine your emotional response. The more negative filters we have, the more "muddy" our picture gets.

As John and I realized that we were stuck in this confined space without fresh air, dependent on the momentum of the line ahead that included senior-citizen ladies unable to fit through the passageway, we started to panic.

We forgot about the two super heroes that voluntarily embarked upon this submarine laughing and posing for pictures as if on a major cruise ship. I also forgot about my belief "I got this." And conveniently forgot to look at the boarding restrictions!

What I discovered that day was that we all have a sweet spot emotion that will get us out of a pinch. For us, it was laughter through stating the obvious. There are many emotions that we are capable of feeling every day. In fact, there are a variety of different emotions available, but usually we tend to stick to the few that are our *Emotional Home*. These are the emotions that you mostly frequently operate from.

Consider the emotions that you typically "live" in regularly. Which are your emotional home? Fear, grief, depression, guilt, unworthiness, insecurity, jealousy, hatred, anger, blame, worry, stress, doubt, overwhelm, pessimism, boredom, contentment, hopeful, optimism, expectation, enthusiasm, passion, joy, empowerment, freedom, love, appreciation?

Do you have more negative versus positive emotional home emotions?

Do you experience similar amounts of positive and negative emotions?

If you could choose the emotions and the feelings that you wanted to live by moving forward, which would you choose?

What emotions do you want to operate from while living your purpose?

How do you want to feel every day? Declare those as your *Sweet Spot* emotions.

Only you have the power to create the experience and emotions that you want to feel daily. It just depends on how you want to show up.

Make note of your sweet spot emotions as a resource towards living your birthright destiny despite any challenges. Try to bring yourself to feeling those emotions daily.

Ask yourself:

Who do I need to become, and how do I need to show up in order to feel my sweet spot emotion?

Now let's throw you a curve ball. Let's consider that you follow the steps and are feeling your sweet spot emotion, but it only lasts 45 minutes because you hit unexpected traffic on your way to a business meeting where you are expected to deliver a proposal to investors for your business. And you know that they operate with a global belief that *time is money*.

Worry and profanity might replace your sweet spot emotion. So the challenge is getting back to your sweet spot emotion despite your undesirable circumstance?

For example shifting:

Worry ➜ Passion

If you want to shift your feelings of worry to passion, then you need to shift your focus. You will need to discipline your thoughts and consciously focus your attention on what makes you feel passionate? *What does passion feel like, look like or sound like?* Remember a time when you felt passionate. Who do you need to become to feel passionate instead of feeling worried while stuck in traffic on the highway? How would a passionate person show up to that meeting despite their tardiness?

Small shifts in your mindset will greatly change the quality of your life. Make a commitment to utilize your sweet spot emotions on a consistent basis. It is a resource that is valuable to maintain empowerment and happiness while finding and living your purpose.

Your Beliefs

Your beliefs have the most impact on your destiny. Your experience of life is directly related to your beliefs because they shape your thoughts and decisions.

The most common limiting beliefs that I have encountered with clients wanting to live their purpose are their beliefs about money and self-worth. "I can't make a living doing what I'm passionate about, " or "That dream is out of reach, and not meant to be for me."

Finish the following sentences:

"Life is _____."
"Men are _____."
"Women are _____."
"The world is _____."
"Relationships are _____."
"Time is _____."
"Wealth is _____."

Your global beliefs are the generalizations that you make regarding broad topics. Our beliefs about these topics will shape how we respond to them. You might want to notice which generalizations you've made have a negative connotation and if you have associated problems in your life related to that topic. Can you identify any internal conflicts? Do you want something but have a global belief that contradicts or doesn't support it?

What belief do you need to have instead to manifest it?

What are *your* global beliefs regarding Living with Purpose?

Purpose means…

_____

_____

_____

_____

Fulfillment is…

_____

_____

_____

_____

Passion is….

_____

_____

_____

_____

Identity beliefs are the beliefs that describe how you perceive yourself. These consist of your beliefs about who you are, what you're capable of and how you distinguish yourself from others.

What have your life experiences prepared you to do?

_____

_____

_____

_____

What are you meant to do? What do you think you were created to do?

_____

_____

_____

_____

What responsibilities do you enjoy doing?

_____

_____

_____

_____

What drains your vitality?

_____

_____

_____

_____

What past experiences gave you a sense of purpose?

_____

_____

_____

_____

What have your life experiences told you about your destiny?

_____

_____

_____

_____

If you had to guess, what is your purpose?

_____

_____

_____

_____

By pulling these strings and finding what is at the other end you will have powerful realizations about yourself, what you should be doing, and what you can be truly passionate about. You will, perhaps even for the first time, be discovering your own *values*.

Values

To live a life of purpose and passion you need to identify the values that you want to uphold and live by in your future. Your values are like the blueprints of your life. They define what is most important to you. Consider the values that are most important to obtain to live with purpose.

What is most important to you about living with purpose?

_____

_____

_____

_____

What values represent the kind of person you that want to become while living with purpose? (Examples: courage, confidence, trust, gratitude, focus, passion, intelligence, playful, fun, happy, fulfilled, heath, love, contribution, personal growth, creativity.) List them below

1. _____

2. _____

3. _____

4. _____

5. _____

6. _____

7. _____

8. _____

In summary, using your own resources is a very powerful tool towards finding and living your purpose. It can be one of the most exciting steps to utilize; many people discover an abundance of resources that they never knew they had! Apply the concepts from this chapter and be prepared to be amazed at how many things that might have seemed difficult or almost impossible before are now actually very easy. Splurge on it!

STEP 8: 1... 2... GO!

Decide... Commit...Take Action!

Inspired Insight:
"Live your divine purpose and discover how it fulfills all of your needs." ~ Coach Delina

NOW IS THE TIME when you must bring your ideas into fruition. It's purpose time! It's time to decide, commit and take action. These steps impact the realization of your dreams.

This is not the time to say that you're interested in living your purpose. This is the time to decide that you're committed to living your purpose.

~

"There's a difference between interest and commitment. When you're interested in something you do it only when it's convenient. When you're committed to something, you accept no excuses; only results."
~ Ken Blanchard

What was the purpose of buying this book? Maybe you were forced to get it, but if you got this far into it, nobody is forcing you now. What were you hoping to get out of it?

The first step you took was deciding to give it a try and open it. The second step you took was committing to yourself by reading it. Whether it was for personal growth or for *Aha* moments, the commitment to yourself and your efforts should be celebrated thus far.

It takes courage to go within. It especially takes courage to consider making changes in your life that do not necessarily comply with your current life conditions. I challenged you hard, we went deeper and deeper to reveal your essence and truth, and you persevered with courage. I appreciate your courage and all of your efforts so far.

YOU ROCK!

Now you can decide, commit and take action towards living your purpose.

Step #1

If change is required in your life, then you must first decide that change is a must. Don't think, "I should change," think "I must change!"

When you leave room for doubt and indecisiveness then you are leaving room for procrastination and procrastination is the anchor that halts forward progression and change.

Change happens when it is a must. If it's regarding your divine purpose and you don't decide to change, then the universe has unpleasant ways of pushing you outside of your comfort zone in order to get your attention – the message being that now is the time. Consider getting fired one of those universal pushes towards your divine purpose. Now is the time!

When you decide and take this first step, you need to declare it and take consistent momentum forward; no turning back.

> *"If you want to take the island - burn the friggin boats!"*
> ~ *Anthony Robbins*

This is one of my favorite quotes because it made me realize my lack of full commitment in certain areas of my life. It means that once you make a decision, put yourself in a position where you can't turn back. I need to start burning some boats, how about you?

For many, deciding is the hardest step because it starts the clock. The moment you make a decision you are drawing the line in the sand and declaring what you stand for, your choice, your resolve.

Making decisions and coming to a definitive conclusion is not everybody's strength. The irony is that being indecisive and lacking clarity is equally frustrating. Most of my clients come to coaching because of their indecisiveness. This is a common problem that prevents people from achieving their goals.

It's not uncommon for people to wait until the pain is unbearable before they make change a must. Everybody's pain threshold is different. Some require very little pain and others require retching pain before taking action. Where is your pain threshold? How much pain can you endure before change becomes a must?

The decision to change is an action step in itself and should be celebrated. You should be celebrating every decision you make towards positive change. Your celebration will reinforce further action. Acknowledge how awesome you are with a mini celebration dance; shake your butt- you deserve it.

Jump up and down and shout, "Yes!"

Look in the mirror and say, "You rock!"

Step #2

The second step is to commit. This involves commitment to your outcome, commitment to yourself, and commitment to those that you're meant to serve. This is the step of "burning the friggin boats."

If you are a commitment-phobe, then this step might cause you some palpitations or angst. I understand, I have difficulty here too. In this case, the decision has already been made but you have difficulty fully committing to it. So you're one foot in and one foot out. You might also have the tendency to change your decision frequently, quickly, and irrationally. Does that sound familiar? If so, then maybe, just maybe, you're a commitment-phobe. I'm not saying that you are, but if we were, then your lack of commitment prevents us from reaching the finish line. And, by the way, you end up stuck like the indecisive person. This is frustrating since lots time and energy have been invested thus far.

Stay committed to your decision. Your commitment is crucial in keeping you focused and will prevent you from falling short of achieving your goals. You have invested too much time and energy thus far not to achieve your desired outcome. Just keep moving forward! Burn your boats!

Step #3

The last step is to take action. If you don't have difficulty with deciding or committing and burning the boats, then taking action might be your hang-up. Plus, when I refer to taking action, I'm not merely talking about taking any action from a "things to do list." I'm referring to taking intelligent, inspired action. There is a difference. I want you to take action that gives you massive momentum while also feeling happy and fulfilled.

Taking massive action towards accomplishing a task is not easy for everybody. Some are more conservative and less daring or action-driven. If you can relate then you might consider yourself a responsible person that wants to make sure that your circumstances are predictable.

Your approach to taking action is strategic and careful. You might be highly analytical, and maybe, just maybe, even a perfectionist. I understand your desire to live within a predictable, stable environment, it's called *living within your comfort zone.*

It's all fun and games until your comfort zone gets stretched. People can start twitching, stuttering, and sweating when they realize that they are out of their norm, like a claustrophobic superhero in a submarine.

> *"Life begins at the end of your comfort zone."*
> *~ Neale Donald Walsch*

Taking Intelligent, Inspired Action

Taking intelligent, inspired action requires your intelligent discretion and forethought of the purpose for the action step. It requires you to think about the reasons why those actions are important. Always consider your motivation for the action because usually only 20% of your action steps will result in real momentum towards your goal.

What is the purpose of that action? Why is it important? What will you gain? Who benefits?

If you want to feel inspired to take action, attach emotional words to your reasons why and notice how this increases your motivation.

Taking inspired, intelligent action involves and requires the strict undertaking of the important steps that will have the most impact towards obtaining your goal. Do not get caught up in the "doing" from your to-do-list. That will eventually exhaust you, as it requires reserve energy. Instead, connect to the 20% of steps that matter most by focusing on your reasons why and purpose. This will be helpful for managing your time more efficiently.

A common approach towards taking action is taking, what I call "fluff steps." In my opinion, fluff steps are less relevant strides that consume large amounts of time and yield no reward.

Fluff steps are considered generally safe to take, since they do not create enough change to rattle you. People tend to hide behind them. They will leave you with a feeling of accomplishment because you took a step, just not one that gains momentum.

This will further motivate you to take similar steps sideways. I'm an advocate of taking any step in the right direction, big or small, but fluff steps have no direction. They cause you to go in circles. They lack substance and keep you within your comfort zone.

The problem with staying within your comfort zone is that the goal always resides outside of your comfort zone.

A big deterrent of taking real action is fear of achieving what we want most. There is a certain amount of uncertainty that comes with success and that uncertainty creates fear and inner conflict.

Do I really want to be successful? Will my success mean that I have to work longer and harder to maintain it?

Fears are capable of preventing anyone. Procrastination is how we show up when battling with fears of success or failure. Fluff steps are the typical form of action taken, if any at all, while procrastinating.

What will it cost you if you don't take action?

Who will it hurt besides you?

This is your chance, *right now*. It may seem that you have plenty of time and opportunity to make important changes, and while it may be technically true, sitting there right now connected to me via this book *is special*.

We actually are connected right now and this is not always the case. Tomorrow you might be occupied by a meeting with your boss or your brother-in-law, who does not necessarily worry himself that you are living your purpose with passion.

I am here for you, however, as one who has been there,

done that, and lived – *really lived* – to tell about it. And that's what I plan to do with the rest of my life. So go ahead, I'll wait with a smile as you make the decision you have always wanted to make, anyway, the decision you know you need to make deep within yourself:

> *Decide right now to live a life of passion*
> *and purpose, and to feel fulfillment,*
> *and to help others do the same.*

And if you need or would like to, take a moment and really reflect on your decision, then turn the page…

Congratulations!
I am so happy for you!

*If you did NOT make your life-changing decision,
go back two pages and repeat!*

LIVING YOUR PURPOSE

Living Your Purpose

TO LIVE YOUR PURPOSE is everything this book is about. I hope that you will remember all of the steps in this book, but remember that they all point to one pinnacle concept:

Come from a place of passion and your purpose will be revealed.

We all have the ability to be happy and create a passionate and purposeful destiny. You are fully equipped for everything you need to live your purpose. It simply requires you to go within and connect with your heart's desires and passions. Follow your passions, listen to your heart, speak your truth, and commit to the journey.

If you follow your passions, you will be pleasantly surprised how life unfolds for you. Don't keep your passions dormant.

Don't keep yourself dormant. Joy and happiness come from when we pursue the things that light us up.

You hold the key to your own destiny. You hold the key to your own opportunities and to the life you were born to live. The real question is: Are you ready to unlock and unleash your true power? I think you are!

GET COACHING!

How Does It Work?

If you don't have a Life Coach, I recommend hiring one. A Life Coach is a hired consultant whom helps an individual, or a group of people within a company, make the changes necessary to take their life or performance to the next level.

A life coach helps you:

- Close the gap from where you are now to where you want to be
- Have the clarity about what you really want in life
- Uncover what is holding you back from achieving your personal vision
- Take the action steps needed to achieve your vision by supporting and holding you accountable

COACHING IS A "GAP" BUSINESS. It's my business to close the gap from where you are now to where you want to be. From the start, we specifically identify your outcomes and desired results. Then we get honest to reveal your level of satisfaction in specific areas. Once we see things the way they actually are, we can develop goals and a compelling vision moving forward.

I use your strengths to unlock your unclaimed greatness and my strengths to encourage, inspire and motivate. Identifying purpose and passion with each goal creates the fulfillment.

Accountability is key! I hold you accountable and assist your momentum while making sure that you are upholding to your commitments. If not, then we focus on identifying the limiting or self-destructive beliefs that might be preventing your momentum forward.

My coaching involves a combination of powerful questions, accountability and the use of strategies to guide you down the right path. Coaching is 80% psychology - destroying limiting beliefs and applying the correct mindset. What usually prevents you from achieving your goal is mostly your mindset and psychology, not a lack of strategy. It's usually not a matter of a lack of resources. It is usually a matter of the lack of resourcefulness. I can teach you all the tools and strategies, but without the appropriate mindset, you won't apply them or be consistent.

Resources are readily available. The worldwide web is very convenient. Again, it's not about the resources, it's about your resourcefulness. Do you apply what you have and know? Do you hold yourself accountable? Do you schedule your time appropriately? Do you provide yourself with the structure and organization needed?

Areas of Improvement Include:

1.   Environment / Home
2.   Body / Health/ Vitality
3.   Passions / Interests / Recreation
4.   Friends / Family / Community
5.   Romantic Relationships
6.   Time Management
7.   Work / Career / Mission
8.   Finances
9.   Personal & Spiritual Growth

Steps for Success

The coaching process involves specific tools to help set you on the right path toward fulfillment.

Get Evaluated: To help you get honest about where you are and where you want to be, you'll be evaluated and graded according to your levels of satisfaction in each category of life. This will help you develop a compelling vision and identify any roadblocks, which may be preventing your progress towards success.

Set Goals: Working with your coach, you'll establish both short and long term goals and develop a list of action steps to achieve desired outcomes. Each outcome will be specific, measurable, achievable, and aligned with your overall purpose.

Create Momentum: Your coach will help you implement a strategy and methodology to get you exactly where you want to be.

Celebrate your results: Acknowledging your success is a stepping-stone for moving on to your next goal.

Coaching is designed to be supportive and encouraging. The key is to create synergy and momentum towards your personal fulfillment and success. By working together, we'll unlock the greatness harnessed within you by implementing individualized solutions. Through a step-by-step process, you will bridge the gap to your next level of success.

You can schedule your coaching session in advance by using the following online calendar:

- To schedule and book your 30min coaching session: **https://www.timetrade.com/book/8C9PS**

- To schedule and book your 45min coaching session: **https://www.timetrade.com/book/B5P9N**

- To schedule and book your 60min coaching session: **https://www.timetrade.com/book/5QJJH**

TESTIMONIALS

What Clients are Saying About Coach Delina

"I wanted to thank you from the bottom of my heart. You understand your skills and me as a mentor, coach and spiritual guide are truly amazing. Thank you so much for all your help and guidance. You have a gift and I am humbled by your insight and expertise. I am grateful for your honesty, kindness and compassion. You are gentle, but not wavering from your course to direct and lead me to a more rewarding joyful life. I hope someday I may be able to give you something in return as valuable as your teachings and wisdom.

"With sincere gratitude,"
– Robin Muto

"Coaching with Delina is taking a journey of inspiration, affirmation and determination with a companion by your side that is encouraging, guiding and supporting every step of the way. With Delina's help I have been able to identify where I am work wise and why I am dissatisfied with my current work conditions and have identified where my passion really lies."

-Jane Else

"Delina's coaching style is graceful, gentle and very direct to help me get to the heart of the matter with many, many, many important changes. Millions of thank-you's."

- Meredith Friend

"In the last six years I had lost my sense of self and although I have a fantastic career and an amazing little boy, I felt a deeper sense of purpose was missing. In just a few short sessions I have learned how to begin transforming my life and find my purpose. I am rediscovering who I am and what I want to give in this world - most importantly I am learning how to give it in a way that stays true to who I am. Delina has been fantastic and continues to show me how to get to the truth of any issue - I have laughed and I have cried but every single time we talk I have come away with a deeper understanding of why I do what I do and how to get the results I want in this life! With Delina's help I am truly looking forward to creating an amazing present and future for myself and all the people around me!"

- Sonal Patel

"Working with Delina as a coach is like working with someone who can see directly into you. Her laser focus allows her to ask the exact questions to allow you to see into your own blind spots, and thus be able to shift and grow. Her intuition mixed with practical tools and strategy support you to realize any goals you can dream of."

– Farah Jamani Pencharz

"I cannot thank Delina enough for her ability to refocus me upon opening up and living out of my heart. As the leader of 7 companies, stress would commonly creep into my life and I would be operating in my head all the time. I knew that there had to be more than just contribution. Delina helped me open the possibility of accepting contribution and love into my life rather than just giving it. She is a remarkable person with undeniably powerful tools! Thank you Delina!"

– Dr. Karl Fritz Disque

"I was able to make progress in my life that I thought I could never do. When I originally decided to have a coach, I had very specific and narrow goals. Personally for me, sometimes it's the smaller things in life that I need help with. When I started coaching, I realized how those smaller things were interconnected with bigger areas of my life. I finally understood why I wanted to improve in certain areas but was unable to.

Delina effortlessly helped me to see the benefits of opening up new avenues when approaching a goal. It works! She helped me make the transition from where I was then to where I am now. The best part is that Delina understands me. I think coaching with Delina helped me to understand myself in a much deeper way, to respect myself and to take action."

- Olena

"Delina has helped me raise my life and my internal well being to a whole new level!! I have found the love of my life!!!! I have gotten rid of anxiety and fears to be the real ME! I have amazing peace, love and gratitude. Now I'm trying to spread the goodness! Love you Delina"

- Lorena Montes

"What to say? I was very skeptical about personal coaching and resisted it for many years. But I now wish that I had done it many years ago, as I wouldn't have lost my fruitful years and energy. I have done more in the last six months than whatever I have done in my last TEN years. Above all, I have got a SUPERCLEAR Clarity, Determination and Plan to do what I love to do and to keep the toxic things away from me so that I can concentrate on my blessings. If you have any questions about Delina, You can please call me/ email me. I am more than happy to recommend her. What are you waiting for? Go and Do it NOW." :)

- Dr. Hema Chandramohan, GP and Founder of www.RoyalAmore.com

"In a world of overly positive, quit your job and follow your passion messages, Delina manages to keep a realist's view. She is positive, assertive and, most importantly, realistic in her approach. I have personally benefitted from her coaching, specifically, from her step by step plan of putting thoughts into concrete action."

- Mike Higbee, PA-C

"The beautiful thing about Delina is how she not only genuinely listens to what you say, but also listens to your silences. It is only through her insights into these silences that she leads you to ascertain the aspects of your life, which lay dormant underneath the surface, anxiously waiting to be discovered. It is through such loving conversations over this past year that I've grown to discovering my passion and my purpose in life. :)

"Thank you Delina!"

- Madeleine Cook

"Inspiring, Intuitive and Enlightening. These are the words I would use to describe Delina and her coaching style. She has this way of tuning into your needs and creating clear action steps that will help unleash your true heart's desires. She presents new ways of thinking, listens intently and leads you into those "ah ha!" moments that open up a door of endless opportunities for growth. She is a true gem."

- Lily Zepeda

"Through coaching with Delina, I have discovered what really motivates me. She has facilitated my own answers by asking the right questions at the right times. It has made all the difference in my life."

- Christina Harjehausen

"I was kind of lost before coaching with Delina. Her powerful questions and passionate way of leading the conversation between us gave me courage to grab live in my own hands. I have started to live my life fully. She is the most supportive person I have known. Coaching with her is fun, yet effective, life changing!"

- Agnes

ABOUT THE AUTHOR

America's Purpose Coach

Delina Fajardo, PA-C, CPC
Physician Assistant
Certified Life Coach

DELINA FAJARDO is a New York based certified life coach, author, and physician's assistant. For the past few years, she's been a Peak Performance Results Coach with Anthony Robbins at Robbins Research International where she is recognized as, "the dust above outstanding." She is a natural born leader.

Fajardo's 15 years practicing clinical medicine at the most challenging levels, including Emergency Medicine and Cardio-Thoracic Surgery, have given her the tools to provide balance and wisdom during crisis situations. Through these and other life experiences Delina Fajardo developed a strong gift to inspire, motivate, and help others find their purpose, passion, and fulfillment. It has become her life's purpose to serve herself and others through Divine love and grace.

She strives to live through her authentic identity, passions and purpose so that she can inspire others to do the same. Her clients are raving fans because of her linguistic representation of simplifying "hang-up" concepts and turning them into easy, tangible solutions.

Delina's life path was not always smooth but it guided her to discover who she is, what she was created for, and the direction she needs to take. Her mastery level training from Robbins, along with her vast medical experience has made her a unique leader within the industry.

Hailed as "America's Purpose Coach," Fajardo is the author of the groundbreaking *Purpose Now* series, including:

8 Steps To Find Your True Purpose: Your Guide To Living An Empowered Life!

Who is This Sex For Anyways? How to Find Purpose, Intimacy & Passion in Your Relationship!

Are we Friends or Acquaintances? Discovering Your Purpose with People!

CONNECT WITH COACH DELINA

YOU CAN REACH ME in multiple ways and even get started with actual coaching using the resources below:

- Web:
http://www.delinafajardo.com

- Email:
delina@delinafajardo.com

- Twitter:
https://twitter.com/CoachDelina

- Facebook:
http://on.fb.me/Coach_Delina

- Phone:
US & Canada: 518-302-1912
International: +442032890985

11103966R00079

Made in the USA
San Bernardino, CA
06 May 2014